Born to Learn

Developing a Child's Reading and Writing

CAROLE S. RHODES
LENORE H. RINGLER

Pippin Publishing

Copyright © 2004 by Pippin Publishing Corporation
85 Ellesmere Road
Suite 232
Toronto, Ontario
M1R 4B9
www.pippinpub.com

Designed by John Zehethofer
Edited by Anne Fullerton
Cover and interior photographs by Seena Sussman
Printed and bound in Canada by AGMV Marquis Imprimeur Inc.

We acknowledge the financial support of the Government of Canada
through the Book Publishing Industry Development Program for our
publishing activities.

We acknowledge the support of the Government of Ontario through the
Ontario Media Development Corporation's Ontario Book Initiative.

National Library of Canada Cataloguing in Publication

Rhodes, Carole S.

Born to learn : developing a child's reading and writing/
Carole S. Rhodes, Lenore H. Ringler; Anne Fullerton, editor;
Seena Sussman, photographer.

(The Pippin teacher's library ; 37)
Includes bibliographical references.
ISBN 0-88751-104-X

1. Early childhood education — Parent participation. 2. Reading — Parent
participation. 3. English language — Composition and exercises — Study
and teaching (Early childhood) 4. Child development. I. Ringler, Lenore H.
II. Fullerton, Anne III. Title. IV. Series: Pippin teacher's library ; 37.

LB1140.35.P37R46 2004   649'.68   C2004-901040-9

10   9   8   7   6   5   4   3   2   1

CONTENTS

. . . .

FOREWORD

As the writers of *Born to Learn*, we feel a connection to you, our readers. With this book, we wanted to share our knowledge of the developing child and how her learning about reading and writing might be enhanced. But as we worked together, we found ourselves with more questions than answers: Who would our audience be? Busy, working parents or busy stay-at-home parents? Anxious parents-to-be? Interested grandparents or concerned professional caregivers? Maybe someone entirely different — or a mixture of all of these?

What does our audience want to know about the young child? Are we writing about things that everyone already knows? How can we possibly address the needs of every individual child? Should we include something special for parents-to-be? For grandparents? Will men and women find this book equally useful?

Some questions we were able to answer. Only you, the reader, can answer other questions. We are interested in knowing who you are and what you find most informative and useful.

As we looked for answers, we got help from many people. We first want to thank the parents who responded to an early survey we sent out to gather information. They helped us to plan the content of *Born to Learn*, and their comments enabled us to focus our writing on common areas of most concern. We also want to thank Dan, Jeanine, Jeffrey, and Joanna, who shared their young children with us and critically read early drafts of this book. To our husbands, Barry and Harvey, who are always supportive and insightful (and sometimes critical), there are no words to express our feelings. Special words of thanks go to our children, Adam, Allison, Jill, Greg, and Rob, for sharing their lives with us and for giving us many insights into how they learned to read and write as they moved from infancy to adulthood.

We want to express our gratitude to Lee Gunderson for his encouragement and valuable comments as our book progressed from a brief proposal to final publication. Special thanks to Seena Sussman, who spent many hours photographing the children, parents, and grandparents who are part of this book. And we are most grateful to Jonathan Dickson, publisher of Pippin Publishing, and Anne Fullerton, our editor, without whom *Born to Learn* would not have become a reality.

And now we would like to hear from you. Please send us your comments and questions. We can be reached though our website, www.ladder-to-literacy.com, by e-mail at carole@ladder-to-literacy.com or lenore@ladder-to-literacy.com, or through Pippin Publishing. We hope to learn more about young children from you and will respond to your messages and letters.

CSR
LHR

. . . .

UNDERSTANDING OUR

PERSPECTIVE

Simone and André, parents of two young children, are thinking about their children's future.

ANDRÉ: When I picked Jamie up from his play date with Scott today, they were sitting on the floor reading a book together. And guess what? Scott was really reading it.

SIMONE: Really!

ANDRÉ: His mother said he'd been reading on his own for a couple of months now.

SIMONE: But he's even younger than Jamie! He's not even four yet, is he? I wonder how he learned to read.

ANDRÉ: I know Scott's mother reads to him a lot, but we do that, too.

SIMONE: Remember when Jamie said, "When am I gonna learn to read like Beth?" and I said, "Wait till you get to school?" Maybe I was wrong. Maybe we should have done more teaching.

ANDRÉ: I don't think so. We're good parents. We spend lots of time playing and reading with the kids. I'm sure he'll do well when he gets to school. Besides, who taught us to read? Our teachers, right?

SIMONE: I guess Jamie will read when he's ready. Beth has done fine, and she wasn't reading when she started school. But she's loved to read and write since second grade, so we must have done something right — even though we didn't exactly "teach" her.

So what is it that André and Simone did right?

Everyone is born to learn. How and what we learn in our early years is critical to future learning — and what parents do to support their young children profoundly affects their future lives as readers, writers, and learners. While you may not be trained as a teacher, you play a vital role in your child's learning, even of "academic" subjects. It is up to you — and to all of us as parents, family members, and caregivers — to provide the foundation for children's learning to read and write in school. And that strong foundation in reading and writing, the emphasis in the early school years, is what's needed for learning about all subjects, both in school and out of school, throughout life. This book will be your guide as you provide the atmosphere and experiences that every young child needs to become a successful learner.

This chapter focuses on how children come to understand the world, and how parents and other adults need to guide and support children's learning. It explores questions like these:

— How do kids learn how to read, anyway?
— How can I make sure I provide good examples of reading and writing?
— How do I answer all those "why" questions?
— How do my child's surroundings affect her growth in learning to read and write?
— Are there times when I should try to teach my child directly? How do I do it?

Our purpose in writing this book is to give you a better understanding of what your child already knows about language and the many ways that you can build on this knowledge to help him become a reader and writer. In our view, literacy includes skills of listening, speaking, reading, and writing that emerge and develop over time, as children interact with adults and other children. And there is no way that learning to read and write begins on the first day of school! Children need to be guided by their parents and other caregivers as they use language right from their earliest days as infants.

In keeping with this perspective, we describe activities that are appropriate at particular stages in children's development. But we always keep in mind that all children are different, even when they're the same age chronologically. The chapter concludes with a section on how best to use the information in the book.

How This Book Came to Be

Several years ago, we were at a conference on literacy, aimed at teachers and researchers. While we waited for the keynote speaker to begin, we started chatting.

CAROLE: You know, I was thinking: We've done a lot of research and writing together, but we've always shared our work primarily with teachers and other university people. We rarely speak to the people who are most important in raising the children that we write about.

LENORE: If you mean parents, we've done quite a bit of reaching out to mothers and fathers at the parent workshops that we've done over the years and the talks we've given in schools on parents' nights. Almost all of our work with parents focuses on reading and writing.

CAROLE: I know, but that's put us in contact with only a very small group of people.

LENORE: What are you thinking about? Writing something for parents?

CAROLE: Exactly. Why not a book? We know the research, we're both mothers — even if our kids are grown up — and we've been involved in children's reading and writing for many years. I think we could tell parents and caregivers some of the things we know are important about the ways they interact with their young children.

We are both college professors and researchers, based at universities in New York state. At the time of this conversation, we were working on a project to analyze our graduate students' "literacy autobiographies" — their recollections about their own early reading and writing experiences. We were fascinated by what they had written. Many of them recalled their favorite books from childhood — particularly the ones that had been read to them repeatedly. A number wrote about the people in their lives who had had an impact on their reading. Mothers were mentioned most frequently, although fathers and grandmothers were also noted.

9

As we were reading and thinking about our students' writing, we began to come up with ideas about what parents might need to know about their children's reading and writing. Our goals for this book included

— Stressing the importance of family members and caregivers in the early language activities that lead to children's growth in reading and writing
— Sharing our knowledge of the processes involved in reading and writing
— Discussing how young children learn about their world and become readers and writers
— Describing listening, speaking, reading, and writing activities that are appropriate for children at different ages
— Helping parents who are selecting childcare to evaluate the reading, writing, and learning opportunities available within different arrangements
— Critically examining the many children's books, videos, and computer programs that are available today

The more we thought about our goals and what we wanted to include in this book, the more we realized that we needed to know more about what parents today were thinking. We designed a survey and drew on our network of colleagues, students, friends, and family to distribute it widely to parents. The survey asked parents to rank the importance they assigned to activities such as "Making playtime a learning experience," "Talking with your infant," and "Planning reading and writing activities for family travel times." And so, this book was formed by our own experiences as educators and mothers, the ideas in our students' autobiographies, and the feedback we received from the nearly one hundred parents who responded to the survey.

What Comes Before Reading and Writing?

Although this book focuses on helping you assist your child with reading and writing, we would be remiss if we didn't discuss what comes before reading and writing — that is, listening and speaking. As adults, we communicate through listening and speaking all the time, sharing our ideas and reacting to the ideas of others. When speakers and listeners know each other well, communication can take the form of "shorthand" speech — even to the point of completing each other's sentences. At other times, conversations are more detailed and formal.

When your baby listens, she begins to attach meaning to the words that she hears. When she begins talking, she figures out ways to share her ideas and tell you what she needs or wants. It is easier for your child to understand the words if she has concrete examples of what the words stand for. Imagine this scene, for example: Jill, aged six months, is waiting to be fed. As her mom, Cara, busily stirs the food, Jill begins to chirp, "Duh-duh. Duh-duh." Cara replies, "Yes, Daddy. Dad-dy." At this stage, Jill may have little understanding of what the word *Daddy* means. However, the next time Jill says, "Duh-duh" when Daddy is home and Cara points to him and says, "Yes, Daddy," Jill will begin to make the connection between her sounds, the word *Daddy*, and the person.

As babies grow, they begin to use language to interact with others, just as adults do. Imagine a grandfather sitting on a park bench, watching his two grandchildren play. Emily, aged 18 months, starts to cry, saying "I want ba." Her grandfather hands her a toy, but Emily throws it down and cries harder. Siri, aged four, volunteers, "No, grandpa, Emily's hungry. She wants her bottle of milk." In this simple example, we see what can be involved in one person understanding another. Siri understood what Emily said because of prior experiences: She had frequently heard Emily use this phrase and knew the response Emily desired.

As adults, when we listen attentively, we are generally putting together our thoughts while simultaneously forming a response to the speaker's words. This interaction between a listener and a speaker, this conversation, is how we communicate. An advantage of listening and speaking over reading and writing is that this means of communicating allows us to see the reactions our words have on others. Speakers use facial expression, gestures, and rising and falling tones as they speak; they notice their listeners' facial expressions and gestures. Listeners can question the speaker and get an immediate response.

Generally, speakers and listeners have a fairly easy time of understanding each other if they have some things in common. Think about the last time someone spoke to you about a topic with which you had no familiarity. A mechanic would easily understand talk about hydrocarbon emissions, torque, and gear ratios, but the average car driver might find these terms unfamiliar and conversation on these topics difficult to understand. And, of course, it is hard to understand someone who is speaking a language or dialect you don't speak yourself.

In the figure labeled 1A, reproduced below, the speaker and listener are very far apart — they have little in common, about either the topic being discussed or the language being used. In a sense, they are talking *at* each other, not *with* each other. Because they share little in the way of ideas, their potential to learn from each other is lacking. In contrast, in figure 1B, both speaker and listener are truly communicating and are sharing many ideas that may lead to new learning.

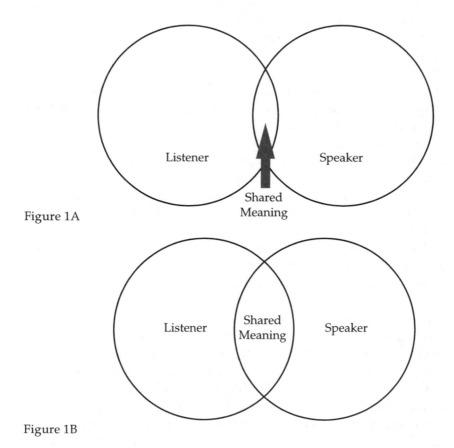

Figure 1A

Figure 1B

Here is a concrete example of how this works. Crissy, age four, and her friend Paul, age five, are playing with blocks.

PAUL: Let's build a city.

CRISSY: OK. I want houses in the city — big houses like mine.

PAUL: We can build apartment houses like yours with the brown blocks. And I want a firehouse and a police station.

CRISSY: How about red blocks for the firehouse? Can we have a park?

PAUL: What kind of park?

CRISSY: You know — a park with swings, seesaws, and sand to play in.

PAUL: Oh! A playground.

CRISSY: Yeah! Let's build a big playground.

In this short conversation, it is clear that Crissy and Paul both have some knowledge of what a city looks like. Crissy may have just learned the words *apartment house* and *playground* through her conversation with Paul, but it is clear that she knew what each was, even if she didn't initially use those terms.

Children gain new understanding and knowledge when they share information, and parents and caregivers always need to keep in mind this two-way nature of a conversation. When adults converse with children, they should try to build on what the children know and should work to expand that knowledge. Parents are always observing their children and know the quizzical looks, blank expressions, and raised eyebrows that can indicate difficulty in understanding. Things for you to think about as you and your child have a conversation include

— What does my child already know about this topic?
— What new information does my child want or need?
— How can I add new information as part of the conversation?
— How can I find out whether my child understands the new information?

Here is a brief example that illustrates how a father notices that his five-year-old son, Aleksandr, did not understand a word he used while they chatted in front of the gorilla exhibit at the zoo.

FATHER: Look at that silverback!

ALEKSANDR: (turning around to look at the man standing behind them) Where is the silver on the man's back?

FATHER: (smiling) No, no — not the man. I meant the big gorilla sitting up on the rock.

ALEKSANDR: Why is that a silverback?

FATHER: Look at the fur on its back. It's a kind of silver color. Some male gorillas are called silverbacks.

The next time Aleksandr sees a silverback, he may use the word. At the very least, if he hears the word again, he will understand it. (All of us understand far more language than we actually use.)

As they grow, children listen and speak about many things with adults and other children. These experiences with listening and speaking help children learn about their world, and so the interactions need to be varied, frequent, and meaningful. Reading and writing builds on the knowledge gained through listening and speaking.

What Comes Next?

Reading and writing are ways of communicating, but they are obviously different from listening and speaking. Writers have an unseen audience: their readers. To understand a writer, a reader needs to be on a similar wavelength. That is, the more the reader knows about the writer, the time and place in which the writer wrote, the language that the writer uses, and the topic that is being written about, the easier it is for the reader to understand the written word.

When the reader and the writer are the same person, the meaning of writing should be completely clear. Take a shopping list, for example. If you have written the list yourself, you will understand it easily as you go up and down the store aisles, even if you haven't described all the items completely. For example, your written list may include the word *soap*. To you, this means a particular brand of laundry detergent for your clothes. But if you give the list to someone else, he may think you want a bar of face soap. On the other hand, if he knows you were planning to do the laundry, he may be more likely to buy detergent (though not necessarily the brand that you wanted). Context helps us to understand.

As another example, consider two readers who bring different background knowledge to a piece of writing. They will probably understand different things from it. Take Diane, whose hobby is fixing up old cars. She will have no difficulty in reading a technical manual on auto repair, while her friend Maria, who knows nothing about how cars work, will get very little meaning from it. However, if Diane gives her friend a simple book about engines and auto repair to read, or encourages Maria to watch her as she repairs an engine, then reading the technical manual will not be so difficult and will have much more meaning for Maria. These readers — like all readers, whether children or adults — bring their background experiences to their reading.

It's important to use books not just to build on childen's existing interests and knowledge, but also to expose them to things that are somewhat removed from their experiences. Exposure to new things and ideas enables intellectual and emotional growth. What is needed, though, is some conversation prior to reading aloud. The key to all of this is knowing your child and what she knows about the world, and being able to provide new information that will help her understand what is being read. For example, a child who lives in a large city and has never visited a farm may have more difficulty understanding the delightful book *Click, Clack, Moo: Cows That Type* by Doreen Cronin than a child who either lives on a farm or has visited one. Children who have seen caterpillars and know something about them will find it easy to understand Eric Carle's *The Very Hungry Caterpillar*, while those who have no familiarity with caterpillars may find the story difficult and not so much fun. In both cases, children who are unfamiliar with the topic of these books need to have a conversation about the animals they will meet and the new words in the story (for example, the word *type* in *Click, Clack, Moo*) before you share the actual story and pictures. This makes reading aloud not just more fun but adds to your child's existing knowledge.

Look back at figure 1B on page 12, and imagine substituting the writer for the speaker, and the reader for the listener. The more overlap between the reader and writer, the easier it is for the reader to understand the ideas of the writer. Areas of overlap could include not only familiarity with the topic, but also familiarity with the language the writer uses. All of this is a roundabout way of saying that new knowledge builds on previous knowledge, and new understanding builds on previous understanding. The way to foster this growth and development in knowledge and understanding gained in reading is by ensuring that our children have varied experiences with books and other reading materials.

Things to Do at Home

SETTING A GOOD EXAMPLE

Do your children see you reading? Do they see you writing? While you may think that babies, toddlers, and preschoolers are too young to share in your reading and writing, you are your children's best role model, beginning right from their infancy. It is not surprising that many children express an interest in what their parents are doing. Children need to see how adults use reading and writing, and how important it is in their lives.

A perfect example is when we read the morning newspaper — even if we don't find the time to do that until evening! When our children see us reading the paper, they begin to understand the idea of reading for information, and they see us using reading to keep informed about the world we live in. While we do not expect a two-, three-, or four-year-old to read with us, there are a number of items in the newspaper that are of interest to young children, and sharing these items can turn the example we've set into a more concrete application. Why not use the television page to point out their favorite program, the station, and the time? Does the same program appear in tomorrow's newspaper? Is it at the same time? Here is an opportunity to examine a calendar together, and to write notes on it to mark when favorite programs are on — not just your children's programs, but yours as well. Advertisements for food and the weather page also provide almost endless opportunities for sharing.

It is also important for your child to see you totally absorbed in reading a book or magazine for a period of time. By observing you as you quietly read, your child begins to understand that reading is a pleasurable activity, a private activity, and one that is important enough that you plan special times for it. Many young children, after observing their parents reading, pick out one of their picture books, turn the pages in a purposeful way, and may even talk to themselves about the pictures. If the storybook is a familiar one that your child has heard many times, you may hear her "read" the book by reciting it from memory. While she may not duplicate precisely all the words on the page, your child may very well "read" the illustrations and know the words that fit that part of the story line. Here, then, is a reading time for both of you.

PROVIDING THE TOOLS OF LITERACY

All children, no matter what their ages, need opportunities to explore reading and writing on their own. The everyday environment you provide in your home is critical here. To foster this independent learning, parents need to make sure the "tools of literacy" are available — drawing paper, writing paper and pads, crayons, colored markers, pencils, magazines, newspapers and, of course, books. Keeping these materials in a special place that is convenient for your child to reach will encourage her to explore. Storybooks — ones you have read aloud to your child, as well as others you have not yet shared — need to be placed in an area that is relatively quiet and private, on shelves that are easy for your child to reach. You may be surprised to see your toddler or preschooler — or maybe even your one-year-old who clearly cannot read — turning the pages of a favorite storybook.

Another item that provides a great and easy way to show the many uses of reading and writing is a large wall-hung calendar. Reminders about play dates, doctors' appointments, visits to grandparents or other relatives, and vacations can be noted on the appropriate dates. Then you, with your child's help, can write stories about the experiences, to read at appropriate times. A family bulletin board can also become the focus of reading and writing activities. Invitations received in the mail can be posted and read several times before the event. Notes to other members of the family and their responses offer another effective way for young children to see how important language is to the adults around them. Notices of important family events, particularly around holiday times and birthdays, become an additional source for repeated readings. The family bulletin board is also an important place for children's drawings and writings. Drawings and simple writings that are brought home from daycare and preschool need an audience and can be posted here — or on that familiar favorite spot, the refrigerator door.

PUTTING PEN — OR CRAYON! — TO PAPER

Drawing and writing are important ways that children communicate with others. The drawing and writing that your child produces needs an audience: you! Children draw pictures of their family, friends, pets, house, apartment, or neighborhood — and other things that are familiar to them. Each of these drawings can spark a conversation. Many times children add scribbles to their drawings. While these scribbles may not resemble your writing, they are real communication. Actually, we call it "scribble writing," and it is the important first step to more conventional writing. You will probably not be able to read it, but usually your child will be able to "read" it to you. Some scribble writing may even contain a replication of one or more letters of the alphabet. Children are generally pleased to read their message to an adult. All you need to do is ask!

Dan, age four, wrote this message and put in on the family bulletin board:

When his father asked him about it that evening, Dan read it aloud: "I played with Jeff today and we fell in the mud." This simple message sparked a conversation: Dan's dad asked him how it happened, whether he got dirty, and how Jeff was. Dan had a lot to tell his father about this event, which was so important to him that he had written about it and wanted to share it with his family.

Here is another example:

When asked what this meant, Allison, aged three, said, "When I go to sleep, I take my bear." Only Allison could read this written communication, and it is important that she was asked to do so. This helps to convey the message that we can write down things that we talk about and read them back.

Adam, a three-year-old, knows that his big sister Esther, almost five, writes in her journal, and he wants to keep a journal, too. Adam made up a story and illustrated it, and Esther wrote things down for him:

When asked about his story, Adam said, "Mommy and Adam went to the store. I love my panda bear."

Away-from-Home Activities

It is almost impossible to avoid print: We are surrounded by it wherever we look. It appears on food packages, on clothing, in the street, in shops, on buses and trains, on television and the computer. What we do with this print can help our children make sense of their surroundings.

Some parents point out print to their children almost unconsciously, while others are more deliberate. Both of these approaches — and a combination of them — make sense. For example, many parents unconsciously say the words "Walk" or "Don't walk," watching and reading the traffic signals as they wait with their children to cross the street. Other parents are more deliberate in their approach and not only say the words but point to the signals, explain that red means stop and green is for go, and talk about why it is important to follow the signs. This extended conversation gives meaning to the words and helps the child to make sense of his surroundings. When you take or make these opportunities for conversation, you will be amazed at how quickly your child begins to read signs for himself.

Shopping provides another excellent opportunity for reading. We all know two- or three-year-olds who can pick out a new breakfast cereal they want from a grocery store shelf. Sometimes television advertising has contributed to their ability to read the boxes; at other times it may be a cereal eaten at a friend's house. Children who recognize labels become partners in the shopping experience. Granted, asking your young child to become your helper at the store will mean you need more time than usual for shopping, but think of it as a teaching and learning activity. When you are in the cereal aisle, ask your child to select a particular brand. The same approach can be used in choosing the size of a milk container, the kind of juice to buy, or the number of apples for a recipe. Even a discussion of which apples are for eating and which are good for baking would be appropriate.

Most of us can probably imagine a shopping experience like this one: A mother and her four-year-old daughter, Yoko, are in the supermarket. It's crowded and late, and the mother is impatient. Yoko keeps pointing to things — balloons, cereal boxes, and sponges — and saying, "I want that." Her mother, being in a hurry, just says, "No, you can't have that." But she does take notice of the fact that all of the objects Yoko points to are purple.

This leads Yoko's mother to follow up the shopping expedition with a reading experience. The next day, she says to Yoko, "I noticed yesterday at the store that everything you asked for was purple. I think maybe purple is getting to be your favorite color! So on the way home from work today, I stopped at the library and got us a book." She shows *Harold and the Purple Crayon* by Crockett Johnson to Yoko and, pointing to the crayon on the cover, says, "Here's something purple. Let's read it together. It's called *Harold and the Purple Crayon*."

This story illustrates how even within our hectic lives, there is time to observe and take note of children's interests. This mother followed up on her daughter's attraction to the color purple by selecting a book that she thought would complement Yoko's interests.

Putting the groceries away is another follow-up to a shopping expedition that can encourage learning. When they help sort items for the refrigerator, the freezer, or the kitchen cupboard, children learn to put things in meaningful categories. This activity can be accompanied by a discussion of different foods and how they need to be stored at home. While this may sound like a difficult concept for young children, it can be simplified if you start with what they know. Almost all young children know that ice cream melts if it is not kept frozen. From this knowledge you can move on to why milk and cheese should go in the refrigerator while canned foods can be kept on a shelf without spoiling.

Traveling in cars and on buses and trains offers many opportunities to explore print. Children can follow a street map to see the route to your destination. They can use transit system maps to match the signs as the bus, train, or subway travels its route. In addition, some of the advertisements that appear on roadside billboards or above the seats in public transportation vehicles make for interesting conversations. "What does that say?" is frequently heard on buses and trains, as young children point to ads that have caught their attention. Parents or other caregivers usually respond either by reading the advertisement, if it is appropriate to the age of the child, or simply by telling the child what it is about. But in helping children to understand any of the print around them, it is important not to just point out examples and read them, but also to give each instance some meaning. As you expand on the meaning of signs, symbols, and labels and extend the child's language as she questions and talks about print in the environment, the world begins to make more sense to her. The child sees that adults are interested in language and that print has a function in our society.

Making the Most of Everyday Opportunities

Let's listen in as Enrique and his four-year-old son, Jose, are getting ready to take their dog for a walk.

JOSE: How far are we going to walk today?
ENRIQUE: I don't know. How far do you think we should walk?
JOSE: How about ten blocks?
ENRIQUE: What made you pick ten?
JOSE: I think that's how much we walked last time.
ENRIQUE: OK. Shall we count the blocks as we walk?
JOSE: I'll count the first bock and then you can count the rest.
ENRIQUE: OK, let's go. I wonder how long it will take us to walk ten blocks. It's 2:00 o'clock now. (Enrique shows Jose his watch.)

This conversation could have been much shorter: Enrique could simply have answered Jose's first question by saying that they would walk about ten blocks, but instead he engaged his son in a longer conversation in which he encouraged Jose to participate. Most of us would not call this teaching, but let's look at the learning that occurred. Jose didn't pick ten blocks randomly; he recalled a previous walk during which his dad probably noted that they had gone about ten blocks. Today, as a result of their conversation, Enrique and Jose have a purpose for their walk in addition to exercising the dog: they will count the number of blocks, and Enrique will probably look at his watch when they return, show it to Jose, and explain to Jose how he can tell how long the walk took. Perhaps the next time they walk the dog, Jose will ask how long they will be out instead of how many blocks they will walk.

Educators call conversations like Jose and Enrique's "teachable moments," and they are invaluable in expanding your child's use of language and his thinking. They do not require planning, but they do require the ability to take advantage of where your child is at that moment, to listen to your child's questions and respond appropriately. The better you know your child, the easier it is to expand his knowledge by using events that actually occur. By listening to and observing your child, you come to know just how much information he is ready to absorb. When a teachable moment arrives, you have a very good sense of how much to teach. Putting groceries away, as described above, is another example of a teachable moment. Such times offer the chance to answer questions, explain something, expand on an idea that your child shares with you, or ask a relevant question of your own.

Just having a conversation with your child is a teachable moment. Almost all conversations can be used to expand knowledge and extend language. Listen to these two different conversations, overheard at a local zoo where two mothers and their preschoolers were watching the tigers.

COURTNEY: The tiger looks a little like our cat!
MOTHER: Uh huh.
COURTNEY: Is Fluffy like the tiger?
MOTHER: I guess so.

JESSIE: The tiger looks like our cat!
MOTHER: You're right. The tiger has whiskers just like Timmy, only longer. What else do you see that is like Timmy?
JESSIE: The tiger's claws are big, but they still look a lot like Timmy's. The tiger is curled up like Timmy, too. Why do cats have whiskers?
MOTHER: Tigers and our cat are a lot alike. Some people call tigers "big cats." I saw a book about cats and tigers in the zoo shop. Let's look at it before we go home. Maybe the book will tell us why cats have whiskers.

These two conversations clearly demonstrate how a child's interest can be either ignored or fostered during a teachable moment. Here, too, it's interesting to note how Jessie's mother answered a "why" question: by suggesting a book as a tool for finding the answer. Other ways to answer the many "why" questions that your child will ask include giving a simple response or going to an authority (in this case, perhaps a zoo keeper or other zoo employee, or sometimes a friend or relative who may be an expert in a particular subject). And it's OK to answer, "I don't know," particularly if it's followed by "Let's see if we can find out." It is good for children to know that there are some questions that you as an adult do not know the answers to.

We hope that by serving as a model for your child, talking about the print that is everywhere around us, answering questions, providing a rich home environment, and taking advantage of all those teachable moments, you will help your child be prepared for learning the important tasks of reading and writing.

Using This Book

We have organized this book according to the usual developmental stages reached by children in particular age groups. But that in no way means that all children will neatly fit into the age levels we have described. Children vary not only in their physical growth, but also in their language and learning development. We know it's natural to want to compare your child to some standard or to another child, but our advice is to try not to do this. Just enjoy your child where she or he is, and know that growth will continue. Perhaps the most important thing we have to say as we end this introductory chapter is that you should relax and enjoy your child. Laugh, play, talk, listen, observe, read aloud, write together and, above all, be sure that you and your child have fun.

We suggest that after reading this first chapter, you scan the table of contents and read the first part of the next three chapters, including the set of questions. By reading these brief sections, you will get a perspective of the whole book. At this point, as busy adults, you may want to select only the chapter from these three that is most applicable to your child, and read that in its entirety. Of course, it is best to read all of the chapters, because in each one there are ideas that can be modified for all age levels. We describe many activities, but it is important to remember that these are only suggestions. Select those activities for which you have time, those which you feel are most appropriate, and those that are of the greatest interest to you and your child.

Those readers who are contemplating choosing a caregiver, selecting a daycare facility, or deciding on a preschool will find the chapter "Caring for Your Child: A Time for Decisions" particularly relevant, and in the following chapter we provide some suggestions about learning materials and other resources. We know that as soon as this book is printed, there will be many, many new books, toys, games, software, and so forth available, so we will provide updates at our website, www.ladder-to-literacy.com. Even if the suggestions offered here in print become dated, an important part of the final chapter is the suggestions we offer about how to select various materials.

. . . .

YOUR INFANT:

BIRTH TO TWELVE MONTHS

Two fathers, Peter and John, are sitting in the playground with their young infants, who are sleeping peacefully in their strollers.

PETER: You know, my wife brought home one of those books made out of fabric for Jimmy. But he's only three months old! I sure don't know what she plans to do with that book.

JOHN: Oh, we have three or four of those little books in the house. I just bought a new one yesterday. Jamal loves them.

PETER: What do you mean he loves them? He doesn't really understand what you're saying when you read them. Does he?

JOHN: Well, Jamal loves to sit with me or my wife while we read the words, and he sometimes seems to be looking at the pictures. The other day he even picked one up, and it seemed to me as if he was trying to open it.

PETER: Well, it seems like a waste of time for me to read books with Jimmy. Maybe when he's older.

Like Peter, many parents and caregivers don't see the point of reading aloud to very young infants. John, on the other hand, seems to value the time he spends with his son as they look at a fabric book together. Although we agree with Peter that Jamal does not understand the words that his father reads to him, it is an important sharing time. It is critical to remember that infants are constantly learning, and it is the adults around them who make this learning possible. Interacting with our young children, whether by reading aloud or talking about everyday things, provides important learning experiences.

27

In this chapter we focus on the first year in the life of a child. This is a period of enormous growth, during which infants learn how to live with the objects and people they encounter. We describe what and how the young infant comes to know about his world, with a specific focus on language. We also discuss activities for you to do with your child, including reading aloud, playing, and observing signs of language development. Through such activities, you help your infant learn more about his environment and about language.

Here are some questions to think about as you read this chapter:

— How does language develop?
— How does my infant learn about the world?
— What is so special about talking and playing with my infant?
— Why should I read to my infant?

Experiencing Language

Crying can be considered the beginning of language, since it is the best way that an infant has of communicating his needs. When your infant cries, he may be telling you that he's hungry or just needs to be cuddled. Often, a child's primary caregiver will begin to recognize different sorts of cries and their individual meanings: crying because of a tummy ache can sound very different from crying because something is too hot or too cold. When infants cry, they are saying in their own way that they need you. As you respond to your infant's communication, he begins to understand that he can make things happen and that you are dependable.

Once your child passes the newborn stage, she will begin to experiment with ways of communicating in addition to crying. We have all heard infants babbling, which starts with making sounds common across many languages. Gradually, the infant begins to imitate only the sounds that she hears most often. So, for example, a child growing up in a Chinese-speaking environment will soon stop making the sound *vee*, since that sound doesn't occur in the Chinese language.

At about six to ten months, a child's babbling begins to combine vowels and consonants. This may lead you to think that sounds like *mama* and *dada* are first words, but this is not necessarily true. It could be that your infant has merely stumbled on a babbled vowel-consonant combination to which you are assigning meaning. But when you reinforce the child's communication with a response — for example, you might say, "Yes, that's your *dada*, your *daddy*!" as you point to him — she begins to learn more about language. By about eight months infants also make sounds such as whining and grunting. These sounds, combined with babbling, crying, and gestures such as pointing, are an infant's way of communicating with you at this stage. You will certainly be able to understand your infant a good deal of the time, though the communication is not always clear — particularly to those who do not spend a lot of time with your child. We are sure that you are familiar with the scenario in which an infant's mother clearly understands what her child wants, but no one else does.

Around the age of eight months, infants also begin to understand the meaning of some words and phrases, although they are not yet able to speak them themselves. If you play the game of "point to your eyes, point to your nose, point to your fingers, point to your toes" with your child, pointing to each body part as you say the words, he will soon be able to play along. You will be surprised at how the number of words your infant understands rapidly increases after 12 months.

Gradually, your child will move from understanding to speaking. The naming of objects is the beginning of spoken language. As you repeat the name of an object, your infant learns to link that sound or word with the object. For example, your infant may begin to say "ba" whenever he sees his bottle. If you respond by giving him his bottle, the sound *ba* will have a shared meaning for you — even though *ba* is not a real word. Soon your infant learns that every object, action, and so on has a name.

The words or vocabulary that your infant acquires may be quite different from the vocabulary of a friend's or neighbor's child. This happens because infants attend to words and phrases that are linked to what they are doing or thinking. Common first words include the names of important people (*mama, dada,* siblings' names), food, body parts, pets, favorite toys, and actions such as "up" and "bye-bye."

Using the Five Senses

Just as adults use their five senses to recognize and understand the environment and the people in it, so too do infants learn about their world through looking, listening, touching, smelling, and tasting. It is with their senses that infants begin to understand the people and events around them.

LOOKING AT THE WORLD

Everything that your infant looks at is new to him. He will respond to color, movement, shapes, and shades of light and dark. For the first two months, he will focus best on objects that are very close — about the distance your face is from him during feeding time. In fact, your face is one of the most important things that your infant sees frequently, and not only will he recognize you by it, but he will distinguish the different expressions that you make. By about three months, almost all infants distinguish a parent's face from that of a stranger, and even very young infants know the difference between happy, sad, and surprised expressions on the face of an adult. Infants may even be capable of imitation. For example, if you pout, your infant may make a similar face. Interestingly, if you hold your face still, it may appear to disturb your infant.

As parents, we all anticipate the day when our infant first expresses happiness with a smile. Before about 12 weeks, smiles seem not to be responses: Infants at this age smile at things or people they see or hear without any differentiation. It is not until about three months that your infant will respond to you as you smile at him. This social smiling occurs when your infant's visual capacity has increased and he is able to focus his eyes on you and so respond to your smile.

Beginning at this stage of development, looking at objects becomes an important part of your infant's growth. Some infants as young as three or four months realize that hidden objects do not cease to exist just because they cannot see them. By about nine months, they are able to keep in mind the location of an object that has disappeared from sight and try to move so they can reach for or grab it.

Since the infant is interested in observing the world and the people in it, we need to provide objects for her to look at and create opportunities for her to interact with adults and older children to take advantage of her curiosity. For the young infant, toys in bright or strongly contrasting colors (black and white, for example) are ideal. Remember to hold them close to your infant, so it is easy for her to see them. Mobiles with objects in different colors and shapes, hung over the crib at a safe distance, are an excellent infant toy. There are countless mobiles available in stores, but they can also be made at home from colored paper and string. Playing tracking games, in which you move an object slowly from side to side while talking to your infant about what you're doing, is a fun activity for her. Hiding a familiar object — behind your back, for example — and then making it "reappear" takes advantage of your infant's growing abilities. Through these sorts of activities, your infant will begin to understand the objects around her. She will also be looking at the expressions on your face and learning to "read" them — an ongoing learning experience.

HEARING THE WORLD

Infants are very sensitive to sound. Even before birth, they hear their mother's heartbeat, a sound that remains very soothing to them in the days and weeks after birth. By about one month, they can connect sounds with their sources. Their favorite sound is the human voice, and your voice will probably be one of the first things to produce a smile. Even newborns seem to prefer their mother's voice to the voice of an unfamiliar female.

Young infants can distinguish changes in tone, loudness, length, and location of sounds. Since your infant is tuned into the sounds in his world, take advantage of this by talking to your baby often. Answer your infant's coos, smiles, and gurgles with sounds and words. Repeat the sounds that you hear your infant making. Other activities include singing lullabies, reciting simple nursery rhymes, and combining hearing and other senses in games like "peek-a-boo" and "pat-a-cake." A simple talking-and-touching game begins with you asking, "Where is your foot?" Then, touch your infant's foot and say, "There is your foot." Repeat this several times, using different parts of the body.

Be sure to note what kinds of sounds your infant likes best. Some infants prefer soft melodies, while others like music with a strong beat. And remember if your infant turns away when you are talking or singing, he may be saying, "I want a quiet time now." Some infants naturally prefer a quiet environment, while others prefer a noisy one.

TOUCHING THE WORLD

Infants use the sense of touch to explore objects around them. You can supplement this exploration by talking with your child as he investigates, naming the objects he is touching and describing their characteristics.

Putting things in their mouths is one of the early forms of touching infants use to recognize objects. The way an object feels in the mouth (rough or smooth, hard or soft) helps the infant learn about it. Some infants put everything you hand them in their mouths, while others may just look at objects or bang them. But remember to be safe and avoid choking by making sure that all objects around your infant are too big for him to put entirely in his mouth.

The more your infant grows, the more he learns by using his hands to touch things that are nearby. Although infants can grasp things that are placed in their hands, they typically don't begin to reach for things until about three months of age. Offer your baby toys with lots of handles or other things that make holding easy. They should also be light enough for your infant to lift and move around. By five or six months, infants can use their hands to examine objects more carefully. They may touch the surface to distinguish small details and move an object from hand to hand to determine shape and size. At about nine months, infants begin to distinguish between categories of objects — for example, they will begin to recognize the difference between objects that are round or square.

Just as infants need to touch objects to learn about their world and to hear the words that identify them, so too do they need your touch. Stroking, cuddling, and holding her close are all ways of saying that you care.

TASTING AND SMELLING THE WORLD

Perhaps when we think about how our infants learn, we do not think of smelling and tasting as easily as we think about hearing, seeing, and touching, because these two senses prompt less of a reaction for us to observe. But newborns do have a well-developed sense of smell: They are sensitive not only to odors in general, but they can tell one odor from another. Infants' sense of taste is also acute. Newborns can differentiate sweet, sour, bitter, and salty flavors. When you introduce solid foods, you may notice your infant making certain facial expressions in response to different tastes. Sweet tastes appear to have a particularly calming effect — but don't overdo giving an infant sweet things!

You can use your infant's developing senses and knowledge of language by making sure to attach words to different smells and tastes. How often have you said to your infant, "Does that taste good?" or "Isn't that nice and sweet?" We use language for the smells and tastes around us all the time. Even though you do not expect a verbal response from your infant, using words to express your thoughts is always a plus: not only does your child begin the process of learning about language by listening to you, but the sound of your voice is a reward on its own.

Talking to Your Infant

We talk to our infants from the moment they are born. And why not? Talking evokes responses. As adults we use language all the time to communicate with others. So why not use language to communicate with your infant? Infants will respond in their own ways. At one or two months, your infant will coo; by four months, she will probably begin to babble and reach out. By five months, infants seem to recognize the sound of their names.

Very often we use "baby talk" when we communicate with infants. We tend to raise the pitch of our voices, exaggerate intonation, speak in shorter sentences, repeat the sounds infants commonly use to name objects ("wawa" for *water*, for example), and pause longer between our utterances. Infants seem to know the tone of these communications and respond. However, if you feel silly or are uncomfortable using baby talk, then use actual words rather than repeating infant sounds. You may also want to repeat the infant sound followed by the actual word ("baba" followed by "bottle," for example). Whatever you decide to do, remember that the more you talk to your infant, the more responses you will get.

This two-way communication increases as your infant grows and reacts to the world around him. By eight months, infants start to indicate what they want by combining sounds like whining and grunting with gestures and looks in a certain direction. Sounds may be used to show emotion (for example, crying from loneliness or boredom) or to get attention. Between nine and eleven months, infants begin to initiate communication with adults by showing or giving them objects. If you are willing to engage in this form of communication, your infant will bring you many things — everything from toys to food to mud or lumps of dirt. By talking to your infant during this activity you put words or labels to the objects that are familiar to her and help her begin to recognize and use language.

Before infants say their first words, they are able to understand the meanings of some individual words and phrases. It's always a delightful surprise the first time you say something to your infant that requires an action in response, and suddenly he does what you've suggested. Try saying, "Give me the teddy bear" or "Put the doll in the corner," and watch for the response. The important characteristic of early communication is shared meaning of words. Young children first talk about what they know.

Toward the end of the first year, your infant will probably discover the word *no* — and may begin to use it frequently! You need to be able to tell what your infant means when he says, "No." Does he dislike something? If so, then it is important that you change the situation or the circumstances. Or is his seemingly defiant "No!" a means of showing independence? Or has he just discovered the sound of "no" and repeats it without expecting any response from you? Sometimes young children's words have meanings different from the ones that we usually understand. In some cases it may be helpful simply to distract your child by engaging him with a favorite toy or word game. If you are patient and listen carefully, you will better understand your infant's communications — whether they are cries, coos, gestures, babbles, or first words.

Playing with Your Infant

Although infants do not begin to play with toys in ways adults might think of as conventional until about 12 months, there are many play opportunities for your infant before that age. In fact, playing with your infant will come naturally to you, and won't need to be planned or organized. Tickling, dandling her on your knee, having her touch parts of your face — these are all forms of play. Play can consist of you and your infant exchanging sounds, making faces and observing responses, grabbing and holding fingers, looking at objects of different shapes and colors, moving objects around, reaching out and grasping objects, and dropping objects. (Of course, for dropping objects to be considered play, you need to be there to pick them up!) For the infant, the everyday things that we have in the house turn into toys. Pots and pans, plastic measuring cups, and the television remote control can be favorite playthings.

Playing is also a learning opportunity for your infant, and games that involve the senses — particularly hearing and seeing — provide the best opportunities for learning about the world and learning about language. While having fun is the primary reason for playing with your infant, playtime involves talking to your infant, too. As you and your infant interact, he is hearing new sounds, new words, and longer phrases and sentences and responding in his own way. This two-way communication during play is a natural, unplanned learning time.

Reading to Your Infant

Like Peter, one of the fathers in the scene at the beginning of this chapter, many parents think that reading to infants is a waste of time. Some may even feel silly doing it. But we don't feel silly when we talk to very young infants, even when we know they don't understand what we're saying. Talking to your infant is natural, even though the conversation often feels one-sided! But, as we've pointed out throughout this chapter, even very young infants participate in communication and learn about their world and about language by listening to our talk.

So it is with reading. Sharing books with your infant cuddled in your lap is another way of being physically close, different from feeding time or comforting time. Your voice, which is familiar to him, comforts him in a new way. Reading to your infant combines seeing and hearing — and touching, if you begin with "touch and feel" books. (Dorothy Kunhardt's *Pat the Bunny* is probably the best known of this type of book, but there are many others. These books include paper and objects with different textures for young children to explore with their sense of touch.) The rhythm of the words as you read nursery rhymes or simple stories with repetitive phrases fills your infant's world with the sounds of our language.

Reading to your infant should be an everyday activity, if you can manage it. You need to choose a special, comfortable place where you will not be disturbed. Plan a special time to set aside, even if it's no more than five or ten minutes. Good times to think about are before naptime or bedtime, or after meals. If your infant becomes fussy or restless, this is your cue to stop reading.

There has been an explosion in publishing for very young children, so finding books to share won't be difficult. You'll need only a few to get started, because reading the same book over and over again will become part of the pleasure for both of you. As a parent, you can observe how your infant reacts differently to the same book as he grows. Your infant, on the other hand, will benefit from hearing the same language many times.

For infants, choose books with bright colorful pictures — ideally one to a page. Cloth or "board books" with rigid cardboard pages are more durable than paper books, a consideration since you will probably read the same book many times. Avoid spiral bindings, since your infant may decide to chew on the book. (Because of this, board books are a particularly good choice, as are fabric books you can throw in the washing machine.) Plastic books that float in the bathtub are another possibility for older infants. You might also consider making your own books, with pictures of family members and objects that are familiar to your baby. You can cut colorful pictures from magazines, mount them on plastic sheets, and write a word or short phrase on the page. A page with a snapshot of the family cat with the words "meow, meow" on it becomes something to talk about with your infant as you make the sound and both of you point to the cat's eyes, tail, ears, and so on. For more ideas, see the chapter "Finding The Right Resources For Your Child."

As you read aloud, try to vary your pace and change your voice for different characters in the story. Use whispers, tones of surprise or other emotions, and drawn-out vowels. This variety helps to keep your infant focused on both your voice and the book. As your infant gets older, she will begin to mimic the sounds that she hears. Encourage this form of "playing" with the language. Make sure you are holding the book so your baby can see the pages clearly. Point to the pictures, and stop and talk about them. Encourage your infant to feel the book and to look at the illustrations.

Playing, talking and reading aloud are activities that begin in infancy and evolve through your child's early years and into the school years. While the toys, games, conversations, and books change dramatically over the years, the learning that occurs is continuous. Your child is listening to language, expanding her ability to use language, and beginning to understand how language functions in different situations. There is a special joy in reading aloud to a child and observing her responses. For some of us, listening to another person read aloud remains a very special event, for our language continues to grow and change right through adulthood.

. . . .

YOUR GROWING TODDLER:

ONE TO THREE YEARS

Two mothers, Frances and Beatriz, are sitting in a doctor's waiting room with their young children.

FRANCES: You know, Renee really surprised me the other day. Her stuffed rabbit fell under the table. I didn't think she could see it where it had fallen, but she walked right over and picked it up. So now we play a game where I tell her about things I've hidden, and she finds them. And you know what? She has started naming the things she finds!

BEATRIZ: Greg is also doing things I didn't expect. Last week he answered the telephone when it rang and said, "Hello," just the way I would. And he's not quite two years old! I guess he's been listening to me.

FRANCES: It seems a lot really does happen when they're toddlers, doesn't it? Sometimes I wish I knew what to expect. Then I could probably think up new things to do that would be fun.

BEATRIZ: I get lots of ideas right from Greg. After he answered the telephone, I bought him a toy phone and now we have pretend conversations. He loves it! We really talk, you know? Not like a grown-up conversation, but he says things and I say things back.

This conversation suggests how children at the toddler stage play, think, and learn — and how adults can help in this growth. When Frances and Renee play the game of hiding and finding things, not only is Frances helping her child understand that objects (whether seen or not) remain the same, but

39

she adds the important idea that objects have names by chatting with her daughter during the activity. Beatriz enhances her toddler's language growth in a different way by capitalizing on Greg's interest in the telephone. In both of these examples, the mothers took their lead from their children's actions. Observing what your child does naturally and building on it is the gateway to making the early years a time of both play and learning.

This chapter focuses on the young child who is growing rapidly in her knowledge and understanding of the world and in her ability to communicate needs, ideas, and observations. During the years from about age one to about age three, children actively watch and mimic the adults around them. As they do so, they are learning about their world and about the language we use to describe it.

Think about these questions as you read this chapter:

— How does my toddler learn about the world?
— How do we as parents and caregivers help children to learn language?
— What are some ways to make reading and writing fun activities for my child?

Experiencing the World Through Language

Children learn actively, through participation in and interaction with the world around them. At the toddler stage, children are constantly investigating and observing all aspects of their environment. A large part of this environment involves language. Toddlers are surrounded by language and learn about it through a variety of experiences. They are immersed in language as their parents and caregivers feed, walk, bathe, dress, listen, talk, and read to them. Your voice and the way you use language in exchanges and in routines and rituals will set a pattern for what is to come.

As they learn about their world through observation, toddlers often begin to mimic what they see. Of course, your child will most often mimic the people she sees most often — significant people in her life, like you. If you cook, she may begin to get out pots and pans, and a spoon to stir with. If she sees you writing, she may pick up a crayon and imitate you. If you sing songs, she will likely start stringing sounds into melodies.

Toddlers first attempts at language come when they begin to mimic the talk of the older children and adults around them. While the first words are pronounced very differently from adult speech, they usually represent familiar, concrete objects that are readily identifiable. At this early stage of language development, your child may produce new words rather slowly, but his vocabulary will seem to explode after the first 10 or 15 words. From 12 to 16 months, the vocabulary of the young child expands significantly. He will learn the names of many objects and will be able to identify them in pictures or in real examples. He will then begin to play with language, often taking delight in the silliness of some of the sounds he makes. Lindsay, a 22-month-old we know, loves to add the sound of *y* to the ends of words. She prances around the house, giggling while saying "book-y" or "ball-y." Her play with the sounds of language is an important part of the growth process.

The more your child sees and begins to recognize and understand her surroundings, the wider the base of experiences from which she can draw — and the richer her use of language can become. Taylor, who is a little more than two years old, has often visited his father, a policeman, at his office. Now, whenever he passes the police station, Taylor says, "Daddy police." He has clearly taken note during his visits to his father's workplace, and has made a connection between his father, the office, and the work of police officers. At this stage, Taylor is dealing mostly with concrete ideas, but as he matures, he will move toward more abstract thinking. The more experiences his parents and caregivers can provide for him, the more his knowledge base will expand and the easier it will be for him to build from concrete to abstract concepts.

Providing rich experiences for toddlers does not need to be complicated — even simple activities will help your child learn and grow at this stage. For example, when you and your toddler are playing with stacking toys or blocks, many concepts are developed. Think about all the abstract ideas you introduce just through your natural conversation as you build a tower of blocks:

— Color — "Let's put the yellow block here."
— Under — "Let's try the yellow one under the green one."

- On top of — "I put the red one on top of the green one, but it fell off."
- Next to — "Should we put this one next to the yellow one?"
- Big — "This one is too big."
- Small — "I found a small block to go here."
- Same — "Let's find a block that's the same size as this one."

The critical component here is that the abstract concepts are linked to concrete objects. As the child plays with the blocks, sees you moving them around, and hears language describing the action, her knowledge is expanded.

There are numerous chances for even the busiest of parents to enhance the knowledge base and language experiences of their children. Look at and listen to things together, and talk about what you see and hear. You might say, "I hear a bird. Do you hear the bird, too? Maybe that singing means the bird is happy." Sing songs yourself, either to or with your child. Melodies are meaningful to children at this stage, and they love to hear simple songs like "London Bridge." They will begin to sing the songs themselves, replicating the melody and using their own sounds as they sing. Often these sounds have no relation to the actual words of the song, but this is still a language experience, and it will grow and develop into a more sophisticated form.

When you go out for a walk, point out a dog, a store, or a flower you see. Simply by saying, "Look at the dog," you are helping your child make the connection between that four-legged animal and the word *dog*. If you can, bring along a small tape-recorder. As you walk with the tape-recorder turned on, ask her what sounds she hears. You might notice a fire engine's siren, a bus horn, or a dog barking. When you get back home, play the tape and identify the sounds together.

In our very busy days, sometimes a quick story or rhyme while waiting in the supermarket checkout line is all we can do, but that is still an important contribution to a child's language experiences. Simple conversation can accompany a bath, a walk, a trip to the store, or simply relaxing at home. For example, during a bath, you can identify body parts as they are washed. Try playing "What's next?" As you wash your child's arm, you might say, "What will we wash next? How about your hand?" In this way, you attach names to body parts. After a while, your growing toddler might take the lead and tell you which body part to wash next.

It is often difficult for adults to understand what a one- to two-year-old is saying, and what he means by the words he uses. Babies babble, but toddlers at this age tend to "jabber," using sounds strung together as a means of communicating. The jabbering often is melodic, but incomprehensible. As language acquisition progresses, toddlers begin to point at and name objects. Children at this age also begin to connect names to the people they see most often. Parents or primary caregivers are usually named first, with siblings following.

As children near the age of two, they begin to combine words into simple sentences containing verbs and nouns. Typical speech patterns at this stage include sentences such as "Go store" or "Grandma up." Although you may be tempted to correct the sentence construction, it is important to ensure that communication between you is always positive. Of course it is OK to say "Let's go to the store" or "Grandma loves to pick you up" in response to your toddler's request, but remember that this is a time for your child to experiment and play with language as much as possible and in a risk-free environment, where attempts are celebrated and applauded. Through the excitement expressed by those significant adults around them, children gain confidence in their ability to communicate and will become more interested in language. Show your child how happy you are that he is talking with you. Enjoy the silliness of the words, phrases, and sentences he uses, and realize that very soon he will develop language that is more understandable.

Here are some suggestions for ensuring that your child is immersed in meaningful language throughout the day. These activities can be easily incorporated into even the busiest of schedules.

For the one- to two-year-old:
— Make up or recite silly little poems to your child when you change her diaper, give her a bath, feed her lunch, or play with her. This shows her that language is fun and

can stimulate her sense of wonder and fascination about language and language-related activities.

— Help expand your child's vocabulary by playing "What's that?" — talking to him about things you see when you're out for a walk, running errands, or enjoying picture books together. By using language in these ways, you are stimulating curiosity, expanding vocabulary, showing concrete connections between words and things, and showing that language is an important form of communication.

— Sing songs. Songs are joyful expressions of language and often emphasize rhymes, which delight children.

— Play "Where is it?" by hiding a toy under a blanket or behind your back and, through your conversation, encouraging your toddler to find and name it.

— Use language extensively when your child wants to play a familiar game: "Oh good, you brought me the ball. Let's roll it on the carpet."

— Respond when your child gives you nonverbal messages. Young toddlers often communicate by shaking their heads, pointing to things, or lifting their arms. Talk about what he seems to want to tell you. For example, if your child points to something he seems to want, you might ask, "Do you want me to give you the ball?"

For the two- to three-year-old:

— Involve your child in routine tasks, like grocery shopping. Let your child write shopping lists with you; talk to her as you clip and sort coupons. This can help your child learn some strategies for tasks such as classifying and categorizing that involve higher level, abstract thinking.

— Make a "Guessing Bag." Hide a familiar object in a pillowcase or large bag. Give your child simple clues about what it is: its color or shape, how it can be used, and so on — and encourage him to guess what's in the bag. This gives him a chance to use language while developing deduction skills.

— Stick things on the refrigerator. Magnetic letters that you can use to spell familiar names and places (for example, your child's name, *mommy*, *daddy*, *zoo*) are useful. Paste or use double-sided tape to stick pictures of familiar things on magnets, and display these on the fridge. Talk with your child about these magnetic pictures. Display her artwork, and ask her to tell you about it. Children have fun looking at pictures (real and drawn) and saying the words that go with them.

— Make your own books to share. This can be as simple as stapling together interesting illustrated pages torn from magazines, putting your child's drawings (perhaps with captions you help her write) together in a binder or folder, or using an inexpensive photo album to create a photo essay of your family. If sharing and talking about these books is enjoyable for your child, you might want to do something more elaborate. One mother we know uses the family's inexpensive digital camera to snap photos of her son Kim in action, displays them in large format on a computer monitor, and asks him to tell her what he was doing in each shot. The mother then uses word-processing software to type Kim's own words on the screen as he speaks, not only creating a caption for each photo but showing him quite literally how speech is connected to print. Each photo and caption is printed out to become one page in a book. Pages of your children's favorite homemade books can be laminated (most copy shops offer this service), then bound or simply stapled together (covering the staples in colored masking tape protects fingers from scratches — and makes the book more beautiful). Whether simple or elaborate, children love these homemade books, enjoy looking at and reading them over and over, and are proud to show them to caregivers, siblings, grandparents — or anyone else who is around!

Whatever the activity, however, it is important to keep in mind the developmental, social, and psychological aspects of your child in the toddler years. Be mindful of your child's interests and level of involvement. If he doesn't seem interested in something, discontinue the activity. Don't worry that there's something wrong — we all have preferences, and it is wonderful (though sometimes frustrating) to see this aspect of personality emerging in our children. Encourage, support, and nurture your child's language activities — but, most of all, relax.

Perhaps the most important thing you can do to prepare your child to become a reader and writer is to be a model for her. Research shows that children who read early and well come from homes where reading is valued and experienced regularly. Reading aloud to your child shows her the joy that books bring, provides her with an example of what readers do when they read, introduces new vocabulary, and results in a strong bonding opportunity for both of you. It helps stimulate her imagination and offers opportunities to experience things that may not be readily accessible in her daily life. Additionally, when we read aloud with our children, they get to snuggle up close to us, so they feel loved and connect reading with pleasure.

As described in the previous chapter, listening to books read aloud is a worthwhile and fun learning activity beginning right from birth. During the toddler years, children can look at pictures and listen as we read and point to various objects illustrated in books. As you read, point to the pictures and say the names of the things they show. As your child gets older, you can connect the word, the illustration, and an example of the real object. Beth, who was reading a book about getting dressed to her 18-month-old daughter, stopped to say, "Look! Here's a picture of a little girl combing her hair. That's a comb. Where's your comb?" Beth and her daughter then went to find the comb in the bathroom. "Yes! You've got a comb, too!" Beth commented. "And I love to comb your hair." In this way that was natural and meaningful for her daughter, Beth introduced the abstract idea that pictures and words can connect to real things.

Another meaningful way to make connections between objects and print is to point out written words in your child's world. You can point out signs at the park, at the zoo, or when you're out walking, shopping, or driving. When you visit the zoo and stop to look at and talk about the lions, for example, point out the word *lion* on the sign displayed on the enclosure wall or fence. This will help your toddler connect the spoken word to the written word and to the actual animal. You could follow this up by looking for a book about lions at the zoo shop or your local library, showing him the pictures and reading the text — while pausing occasionally to talk about your zoo visit. Similarly, when you are in the supermarket, your child is surrounded with labels that represent concrete, familiar objects. Make this into a learning experience by pointing familiar ones out to your child. Even young toddlers recognize the names and logos they see often on favorite foods.

Parents often ask how to pick the best books for their children or for tips on the best way to read aloud. We're always happy to reply that there's no best book or correct way — it's the experience of being read to that is significant for the child. It doesn't matter if you read greeting cards, nursery rhymes, songs, cloth and tub books, or bright picture books. What is important is conveying the idea that printed material can provide pleasurable experiences. (When you do use cardboard or cloth books, be aware that, at this point, your toddler might enjoy looking at, tossing, or chewing the books more than being read to!) Point to the pictures and name the objects. Ask your young child to point at and name things, too. Keep books, magazines, and newspapers around the house, and let your child play with them.

Sometimes a good book selection is suggested by an activity you might be planning. For example, if you're taking a short trip to a new place, you could find a book about that place and share it before and after. Books can also be connected to familiar activities. Before you go to the playground, for example, you might want to look at *Maisy Goes to the Playground* by Lucy Cousins. Afterward, you can remember your outing by reading the book again. Additional ideas for picking books and some recommended titles for toddlers appear in the final chapter.

Make reading aloud part of your routine, not something for special occasions or to be used as a reward. Read as often as you and your child have time. If you don't have time to read a whole book, read just a bit. If your routine is too hectic to read every day — and this is true for many of us these days — then plan to read three or four times a week. Too many busy parents feel that they *must* read to their child every day, and then it becomes one more task rather than an experience that is relaxing and fun for all concerned. The important thing is to have a positive experience sharing language and time together.

It is helpful to set a good tone and mood before beginning to read, by giving your toddler and you time to settle down. For all children, reading stories before bed makes a good transition between active play and rest time. One mother we know always stops reading at a very exciting or enjoyable point in the story so that she and her child will eagerly look forward to the next read-aloud. At this age, reading time is physical and social as well as intellectual. Children should be encouraged to talk, point, and follow along as they are read to. Let your child hold the book and turn the pages for you. Talk about the story and what's in the pictures. Be sure to read slowly enough for your child to understand (most people read aloud too quickly), and try to read with expression. Don't be afraid to ham it up! Also, be willing to stop reading if your child no longer seems interested. Above all, it is important to remember that reading to your child should be fun for both of you.

It is a good idea to take even the youngest child to visit the local library. One of Carole's fondest memories of her own early childhood years was when her mother, Fran, took her to the library. Watching her mother select books and seeing the enjoyment that Fran got out of the process told Carole, even at that very young age, that books led to pleasurable experiences. Take your toddler to the library so that she can choose books to listen to at home. Today, many libraries are open in the evenings, so almost all parents can fit a library outing into their schedules and enjoy this activity with their children. Find out about your library's special books and services. Many libraries have programs geared for toddlers. These programs generally encourage participation of parents and caregivers together with their children. They often open with a read-aloud, followed by activities such as storytelling, singing related songs or reciting rhymes, and finger plays.

Experiencing Writing

Many parents these days incorporate reading into their routines with their children, but most think less often about writing. However, writing development happens in similar ways to reading development as our children watch and learn from us. Also, reading and writing development are closely connected and reinforce each other. Think about how often your child sees you write at home: Most likely you write notes to yourself and others, lists, checks, and phone messages. You may write e-mail, reports for work or courses you might be taking, letters, or other, more extensive pieces.

The child of this age is often engaged in role-playing as she experiments with writing tools. She loves to scribble with markers, crayons, or pencils (on paper, we hope, rather than on the walls or furniture!). These early drawings and writing activities are the beginning experiences that will lead to more formal writing later on. They are your child's way of emulating your behavior, but they are also a basic form of communication for your child.

Buffy's grocery list

Stevie is playing with his toy telephone, and he writes a message for his dad.

To encourage writing, keep writing materials — such as washable, nontoxic crayons and markers, paints and brushes, and different kinds of paper — where your child can reach them. If possible, have a small desk or child-size table on which you can place writing materials so that they are easily accessible to your child. Take books and writing materials for your children with you whenever you leave home, so that they can read or write along the way or when you reach your destination. Talk to your child about his writing. Encourage him to read to you what he has written (you probably won't be able to read it yourself, since he is unlikely at this age to form correct letters or to have a sense of spelling conventions). Show your child how you read and write every day to have fun and to get things done.

There are many ways that we can begin to encourage writing as a form of communication. Share your writing with your child. As you write your grocery list, talk to your child about it. You may even assist your child in writing her own list. It can begin with talking about what she wants you to buy at the supermarket and move into cutting out a picture which you label. Your child may simply put a mark on a page or scribble what she wants. Be sure to discuss this with her and, whenever possible, when you take your child to the market with you, be sure to buy what is on her list.

A Word about Teaching Your Toddler — Naturally

For toddlers, learning about the world and the language we use to describe it takes place as they interact with family, friends, and caregivers. While some adults may feel a need to do more formal "teaching" at this stage of development, it is not an approach that we endorse. Drilling toddlers to recognize the letters of the alphabet or teaching specific words is not necessary. The informal teaching that occurs as we talk, play, and read to toddlers is far preferable to any formal teaching.

Of course, the toddler stage isn't too early to begin learning about letters and sounds. Your toddler learns many of the sounds that letters stand for and begins to recognize letters and words in print as you point out the signs in her surroundings and read aloud to her. You will find that there are many opportunities for your toddler to acquire the skills that she will need to learn to read and write later, without explicit teaching at this early developmental stage.

Computers may present an additional concern. Computers for toddlers are not something we particularly endorse. Educational software that purports to teach reading and writing skills is not appropriate for toddlers. Also, computers which are made for young children are often more technically oriented and less "child friendly" than we would like. Buying an expensive, easily broken piece of equipment is probably unwise. If your child does not use the computer or uses it in a way that you don't like (with sticky fingers, for example), an atmosphere that is not conducive to learning may result. It is much better to wait and, if you choose to purchase a computer for your child's use, do so when she is beyond the toddler stage. You can find more about computer use and appropriate computer activities in the chapter "Finding the Right Resources for Your Child."

. . . .

YOUR PRESCHOOL CHILD:

THREE TO FIVE YEARS

Marie and Tamiko are having coffee while the three preschoolers they care for are playing in the next room.

TAMIKO: You know, I'm so glad you were able to come over to-day with Tonio and Giovanna. Robert is a lot of fun to be with these days, but I'm getting tired of answering all his questions. All he does is talk all day! I just say yes or no to most of his questions now.

MARIE: Well, I guess it's easier for me because Tonio and Giovanna have each other to talk to. But sometimes they really want me to answer their questions. Just the other day, Giovanna wanted to know why the leaves were falling off the trees. I didn't know what to say exactly, so we looked in a book she has about the seasons.

TAMIKO: Well, that happens to me sometimes, too. And when I just say yes or no, Robert gets really frustrated with me. It's like he wants more information, but sometimes I just don't have all the answers.

MARIE: Maybe you could try talking to him more — maybe about familiar things, so he won't be so busy asking hard questions. I told Tonio and Giovanna a story about when I was a little girl growing up in the country, and they had a lot of questions that I could answer. We had fun talking about how different my childhood was from theirs. And then they drew pictures of me in the country, and I drew a picture of them in the city.

Between the ages of three and five, children develop an almost insatiable curiosity. It is up to parents, caregivers, and other adults to give them every opportunity to learn as much about the world as they can absorb. Marie has clearly figured out a way to involve Tonio and Giovanna in conversations about things that she is familiar with and in which they are interested. This is an excellent way for any adult to interact with children of this age. Focusing conversation on a child's interests and using stories and examples from your own life provides opportunities to expand the child's knowledge, both of the world and of language. By listening to what children say and observing their reactions to a conversation, we broaden their world and help them to make sense of it. By the same token, giving simple yes or no answers to a child who is seeking information may frustrate her and increase her need to ask even more questions.

This chapter focuses on the critical years before a child goes to school. This is a time in which parents, caregivers, and other adults provide many opportunities for literacy learning. They are tuned into "teachable moments," those natural opportunities for helping a child gain new knowledge and understanding, and they plan for many learning experiences. As children listen, talk, and respond to their world in writing, drawing, or play, they use literacy to organize their thoughts and meanings and communicate them to others. As children see you doing your own reading and writing, they expand their understanding of the many forms of language.

Here are some questions to think about as you read this chapter:

— What are some of the ways that my young child's use of language expands?
— How can I provide many opportunities to help my child learn to read and write?
— What are some techniques for reading aloud to my preschooler?
— What are some good learning activities I can work into the time we spend together?

Understanding the Language Development of the Young Child

As your child grows, so does his ability to use language. Children are naturally active, and this is true of their language learning, too: they learn about language as they use and hear it used in different situations. Researchers believe that language and thinking begin to intermingle at about two years of age, so that children start to use language in their minds as they think about things. At this stage, the child also begins to share ideas and expand them by listening to the language of others. In this way, language becomes intellectual, and thought becomes verbal. The child uses language more intensively to explore relationships with people and things in the environment. Between two and three, children begin to take the listener into account, making their communication more interactive as they learn to say things in a way that makes the meaning clear to an audience. This skill develops slowly until age seven or eight, but even children as young as four have been observed to change their speech when they are talking to younger children: they use shorter sentences, they speak more slowly and with simpler words to make it easier for the younger child to understand them.

Just as the preschooler adjusts his speech for the toddler, as parents and caregivers we need to keep our children's developmental stage in mind in our conversations. The developing child

— Asks questions
— Stores information about the way language is used
— Increases vocabulary
— Expands understanding of concepts

During the preschool period, language gradually becomes freed from the immediate, concrete environment, and the child begins to use language to think about and express ideas about people, objects, and events — even when they are not present at the moment. As a result, the child's memory store expands; growth can be seen in the ability to rely on past experiences and in the language used to identify and categorize new objects and events. Listen, for example, to what is revealed about a three-year-old's understanding of the difficult concept of death in this conversation between a mother, Birgit, and her son, Adam. It's the U.S. Presidents' Day holiday, and the two are at home together.

ADAM: Why are you home today?

BIRGIT: Well, it's Presidents' Day — a holiday when we remember some of the great presidents. Preschools are closed, and I'm not working so I can be home with you.

ADAM: Can we watch the great presidents on TV?

BIRGIT: No, I'm afraid not. These presidents died a long time ago.

ADAM: Did they throw the presidents in the garbage?

BIRGIT: No! Why do you think people would do that?

ADAM: I remember you saying the flowers were dead, and then I saw you throw them in the garbage.

BIRGIT: Well, you're right about the flowers. I do throw them in the garbage when they are dead. But it's different with people.

ADAM: How is it different?

BIRGIT: Well, when people die, we have special ways to say goodbye to them.

This conversation illustrates not only Adam's understanding of the word *dead* but also how an adult can expand a child's knowledge by providing information and responding to questions in a way that is not beyond the understanding of a three-year-old.

Everyday life presents many opportunities to enrich young children's language development and their understanding of the world around them. Children learn about language and literacy in many ways. They see that print is everywhere in their world; they take part in day-to-day conversations; they ask questions; they observe adults and older siblings reading and writing. As adults we can provide an environment that is rich in print, create an atmosphere in which asking questions is encouraged, and take advantage of teachable moments to enhance language use.

Besides the many opportunities for enhancing your child's language that arise every day, it is worthwhile to plan particular activities that meet the particular needs of your child and fit in with your family life. These activities do not need to be complicated; many require only a small amount of planning. For example, watching television, shopping together, and playing together occur frequently and naturally in most families, and only minimal planning is needed to turn these activities into opportunities for enriching your child's language abilities. Other activities such as reading aloud, storytelling, cooking together, playing games, and going to the library require more planning. These activities, and others, are described in the remainder of this chapter.

Reading Aloud

Just as it was when your child was a toddler, time spent reading aloud to your preschooler can be a very pleasant experience. To make reading aloud fun for both you and your child, make sure you have nothing else on your mind before beginning to read. If you are preoccupied, reading aloud may seem like a chore — and your child will sense your feeling.

Although most of us have heard about how important it is for parents to read to young children, there is more to it than just reading. A critical part of reading aloud to your child is the conversation that takes place before the reading, during the reading, and after the story is completed. This conversation is what makes reading aloud both a pleasant experience *and* a learning experience. Let's listen in as Mitch reads *Ira Sleeps Over* by Bernard Waber to his four-year-old daughter, Sarah.

MITCH: (before showing Sarah the book) Remember last week when you went to Nicole's house for a sleepover, and you took your fuzzy cat with you?

SARAH: I like Pom-Pom to go everywhere with me. I get to talk to her.

MITCH: Does Nicole have an animal that she sleeps with?

SARAH: No. She has a funny blanket that's all messy looking and she takes it to bed.

MITCH: Well, when I was at the library last night, I went over to the children's section to find something new to read with you. I got talking with the librarian a bit, and he thought you might like this one. (Mitch shows Sarah the book.) It's about a boy named Ira who goes on a sleepover. I guess that's Ira on the cover.

SARAH: Looks like he's got a fuzzy animal. A teddy bear, I think.

MITCH: Do you think he'll take the bear to his friend's house?

SARAH: I guess.

MITCH: Well, let's read some of the story and see if Ira takes his bear to his friend's house. The name of the story is *Ira Sleeps Over*. (Mitch begins to read.)

> I was invited to sleep at Reggie's house. Was I happy! I had never slept at a friend's house before. But I had a problem. It began when my sister said: "Are you taking your teddy bear along?"
>
> "'Taking my teddy bear along!" I said. "To my friend's house? Are you kidding? That's the silliest thing I ever heard! Of course, I'm not taking my teddy bear."

Ira says he has a problem. Do you know what a problem is?

SARAH: It's like when you don't know what to do.

MITCH: That's right. I wonder what Ira's problem is.

SARAH: I dunno.

MITCH: OK, let's see if we find out when we read more.

> And then she said: "But you never slept without your teddy bear before. How will you feel sleeping without your teddy bear for the very first time? Hmmmmmmmm?"
>
> Oh oh. I can imagine how you'd feel without Pom-Pom!

SARAH: Yeah. I'd be really sad. I bet Ira will be sad, too.

MITCH: I think so, too. Let's turn the page and see.

SARAH: (pointing to the cat) Look, Ira has a real cat — mine's only a toy cat. Why can't we have a real cat?

MITCH: Maybe, when you're older.

SARAH: And I'll take care of it.

MITCH: "I'll feel fine. I'll feel great. I will probably love sleeping without my teddy bear. Just don't worry about it," I said.
"Who's worried?" she said.
Well, Sarah, I guess we were wrong about Ira feeling unhappy

SARAH: I would be sad without Pom-Pom.

MITCH: Maybe Ira will change his mind.

> But now, she had me thinking about it. Now, she really had me thinking about it. I began to wonder: Suppose I

"I'll feel fine.
I'll feel great.
I will probably love sleeping
without my teddy bear.
Just don't worry about it," I said.

won't like sleeping without my teddy bear. Suppose I just hate sleeping without my teddy bear. Should I take him?

SARAH: I think he should take him.

MITCH: Why?

SARAH: 'Cause I take my cat when I go to Nicole's house to sleep.

MITCH: "Take him," said my mother.
"Take him," said my father.
"But Reggie will laugh," I said. "He'll say I'm a baby."
"He won't laugh," said my mother.
"He won't laugh," said my father.
"He'll laugh," said my sister.
I decided not to take my teddy bear.
Do you think Ira will miss his teddy bear?

SARAH: Mmmmm.

MITCH: Now I think we know Ira's problem.

SARAH: He doesn't know if he should take his teddy bear or if he shouldn't take it.

MITCH: You're right. And it looks in this picture like he's still not sure.

This excerpt of a conversation between parent and child demonstrates several techniques you can use with children of this age to add learning experiences to the pleasure of reading aloud. These techniques, which are useful regardless of what you have chosen to read, include the following:

— Ask a question and have a brief conversation before beginning to read. The question should focus the child's attention on the story, and get him ready to listen attentively. Ask him to predict what the story will be about, or use Mitch's approach and ask something that will relate the story to the child's own experience.

— Stop reading to answer your child's questions.

— Stop reading at critical points either to clarify or to elaborate on something in the story.

— Stop reading to talk about a character and how that character and things in the story make you and your child feel.

I decided not to take my teddy bear.

- Stop reading to ask a question about the story and what may happen next. Then, read on to see if the prediction was accurate.
- Stop near the end of the book to ask your child how the story might end.

When you finish reading the book, the conversation may focus on one or more aspects of the story. Any of the following questions can spark an engaging discussion with your child. Remember that these questions are supposed to begin a conversation, in which you participate as well. Be ready with your own answers, and your comments and reflections on your child's point of view.

- Did you like the story? Why?
- Was there a character you especially liked? What about one you thought was mean or scary? Or one that you just didn't like at all?
- Was there a part of the story that you especially liked or disliked? (You may choose to reread the part that was especially liked.)
- Did the story end the way you thought it would?
- Did you like the ending? Why?
- If you wrote this story, would you give it a different ending?

If you have time and your child is interested, you can encourage him to draw a picture, write some comments, or act out parts of the story in response to the reading.

Reading aloud has advantages other than the obvious ones of helping children expand language and extend knowledge. As your child observes you reading, he is internalizing many of the conventions of book reading and print. As he shares more and more read-aloud times with you, he will begin to notice (and you can begin to point out) that books have special covers, that the title of the story is on the cover and on the inside page, that the name of the person who wrote the story is also on the cover and the inside page, that the pages are turned in order, that the print is read from left to right. While we may not talk explicitly about book and print conventions with children of this age, they tend to be keen observers and may have questions for you. As in other situations, answer his questions at the level that you think he can understand. For example, if your child notices the date 1998 on the copyright page and wants to know why it's there, you could simply tell him that this is the year that the story was written.

Whether your child is three, four, or five, reading aloud to her will be a similar experience throughout this preschool stage. It is a private time between an adult and a child, a time that is planned and uninterrupted by others. The place selected for reading may be a quiet corner of a room, the floor, the bed, or an especially comfortable chair. It's a time for sitting close together, sharing an experience, and enjoying each other. Some parents prefer reading aloud just before bedtime, but this is a personal choice. We know some parents who, when they read aloud just before their child's bedtime, tend to fall asleep before the child!

Perhaps the one difference in reading aloud as your child moves through the preschool years will be the choice of books to share. Attention spans begin to lengthen (though they are still quite short) during this time, and you may move from simple picture books to longer stories. Choosing the right book to read to your child can be a part of the experience. Very frequently your child will know exactly what book she would like you to read aloud; often it is a book that she knows well and has heard many times. This repeated reading of familiar books creates an atmosphere of confidence. She knows what will happen next, and she may even decide to "read" along with you. The local library, your child's teacher, and friends are all good sources of recommendations for read-aloud books. Some favorite books for various age ranges are listed in the last chapter.

Storytelling

Storytelling is often a personal activity in which you make up a story about characters that your child is familiar with. These stories can be about the child, a friend, a member of the family, or yourself. Your child may be very interested in hearing stories about your own childhood, particularly what happened to you when you were the same age as your child is now. You may also have stories that have been told in your family for generations. Of course, these are wonderful to share and for maintaining family traditions. Furthermore, you may enjoy making up stories full of fantasy and adventure. Each type of story for telling is more than acceptable and together they provide you with a variety of possibilities for the storytelling time you set aside.

Stories that you tell should be very much like the stories you read aloud: fairly short, and with a clear beginning, middle, and end. Just as when you read aloud, this is a private time between you and your child, and should not be interrupted. It can be useful to connect the story to something in your child's own life. Here is a story told by a mother to her four-year-old daughter a few days before they were going on a trip to visit the girl's grandmother.

> A long time ago, when I was four years old, my mother told me that we were going to visit my grandmother. My mother said, "Grandma lives very far away and we will be going on an airplane. It will take us two hours to get there." The next day we took a bus to the airport and waited on line to get our boarding passes, so we could get on the right airplane. We gave the tickets to the man at the gate and found our seats in the airplane. I got a seat next to the window. After we were up in the air, a man brought us something to eat and some crayons and paper for me. I made a picture of the airplane and then it was time to land. As soon as we got off the airplane I could see my grandma waving at us. My mother and I stayed with grandma for a whole week. We played a lot of games and had fun. Then we took an airplane back home.

This story has the same structure as a written story (beginning, middle, and end), relates to a family member, and is about an experience the child is about to have. Stories of personal experiences are fairly simple to make up, can be told almost anywhere, and tend to be short. Telling stories like this encourages your child to make up stories about people and things that he is familiar with. For many children, this sort of storytelling is a first step to story writing.

Sharing Nursery Rhymes

Reading or reciting nursery rhymes aloud is different from reading a story. Nursery rhymes emphasize the sounds of words, have a particular rhythm, and are very compact. They contain phrases to chant, silly made-up words that children love to mimic, and repetitive phrases. By sharing nursery rhymes, we help children recognize the patterns and sounds of language. They encourage us to make songs from some of the words or phrases, or to adapt some of the silly words to our everyday lives. By encouraging this sort of word play, we promote a love of language. And, as with favorite story books, reading the same nursery rhyme again and again shows children the relationship between the sounds and the letters representing them. This is an important step in learning to read.

In selecting such rhymes to share, it is important to find those that have rich language and rhythm. If you find a book of nursery rhymes to read aloud, make sure there are illustrations that will help your child form visual images.

Drawing and Writing

Drawing and writing are activities that children can do by themselves, or with you. If she works alone, she will develop the ability to enjoy private time and learn to be more independent and self-reliant — and she will provide you with some private time of your own. Drawing and writing can occur spontaneously if you make sure that paper, crayons, markers, and other tools are available, or they can be specifically planned as opportunities for language development. Generally, for children of this age, drawing and writing activities are best planned to follow some special event. For example, after a trip to the zoo, you might encourage your child to draw a picture or write something about the animals that he saw, so that he can share something about the trip with someone in the family who was not able to come along. Other events that could lead to drawing and writing include birthday parties, visits to friends and relatives, and going to the movies or watching television.

Starting a "family log" of special events provides many opportunities for drawing, reading, and writing. This log, which can be kept in a large notebook, needs to be something that everyone in the family contributes to. For example, if you have just returned from a business trip, you need to write something in the family log about it. It can be as simple as the date and one or two sentences: "Wednesday, September 18, 2003: I liked New York, but I'm really glad to be home!" For a three-, four-, or five-year-old, the family log is a special place to share a special event by writing or drawing something that someone else will read.

Here is a sample of a four-year-old's log entry:

When asked to tell about what she wrote, Esther said, "This is daddy and me. Every day daddy and me go to the store." In telling her story about a trip to the supermarket, she described the man at the checkout counter.

The family log becomes a record of everyone's special activities and can be read and reread many times.

Playing Together

The most important part of playing with your child is to follow his lead in deciding what to play, and then to play enthusiastically. Children of all ages are aware of their parents' and caregivers' level of interest and feelings. Are you bored? Are you waiting to do something that you feel is more important? Are you tired? Are you feeling overworked and out of sorts? If the answer to any of these questions is yes, then it is not a good time to play with your child. But, when the answer to these questions is no, it's time to put things aside and play. Do not answer the telephone while playing with your child, unless you are expecting an important call. When you are ready to play with your child, it becomes a positive experience and one in which your child's knowledge and language can be expanded.

Take, for example, doing a jigsaw puzzle. No matter whether you are beginning with a simple 10-piece puzzle for a young child or doing a 75-piece puzzle with a five-year-old, you use certain types of language that demonstrate difficult or abstract concepts:

— Over — "Let's turn all the pieces over so we can see them."
— Next to — "That piece looks like it fits next to the blue one."
— Top — "That piece fits at the top of our puzzle."
— Bottom — "Try that yellow piece at the bottom of the puzzle."
— Together — "Look, those two pieces are stuck together."
— Turn around — "Try to turn that piece around."
— Under — "Let's try the yellow piece under the green piece."

Children's jigsaw puzzles are also very colorful, and so they provide many opportunities for talking about different colors as well as shapes. With older children, number concepts can also be included as you discuss the number of pieces still to be fitted into the picture.

Board games and simple card games provide many additional opportunities to develop language and understanding related to important concepts. Rolling the dice in a board game is a chance to expand number concepts, for example: first, the players need to count the number of moves to be made on the board; then, as the child's understanding of numbers progresses, she can add numbers when two or more dice are used.

Other concepts involved in board games include the following:

— Same — "We are in the same space."
— Ahead — "How many spaces ahead of me are you?"

- Behind — "I'm four spaces behind you."
- Turn — "Whose turn is it now?" or "Turn the next card over." (Note the two different meanings.)
- Forward — "You got a four, so you can go forward four spaces."
- Backward — "Your card said you need to go backward three spaces."

Card games can develop some of the same concepts. For example, in Go Fish, we frequently use same, different, turn, and ahead. In the card game War, the concepts of higher and lower and matching are critical.

Many children of this age also enjoy dramatic play — make-believe and dress-up types of activities. This type of play encourages creativity and imagination, and provides opportunities for children to use and expand their language. The materials needed for dramatic play are the everyday clothes, hats, scarves, and shoes that you may be discarding. Children enjoy dressing up and then making up a play or stories to go with their costumes. Language is the tool they use to tell these stories. Remember to be an attentive audience for their performances. Since language development depends on communication between individuals, the audience is a crucial component of this play activity. How you react, what questions you ask, and how involved you seem to be are all quietly understood by your child.

Simple outdoor activities such as throwing a ball back and forth also lend themselves to many opportunities to expand language. In playing games of any kind it is important to remember that conversation is a part of the fun. Here are some concepts that may be developed as you and your child toss a ball:

- Close — "You are standing a little too close to me."
- Closer — "Come a little closer to me."
- Back — "Move back a little bit."
- Together — "That's great! Keeping your hands together that way really helps you catch the ball."
- Apart — "See how my legs are apart. Can you try that?"
- Far — "Oops! That was a pretty bad throw. I really threw that ball far away from you."

More Opportunities for Using Language

SHOPPING TOGETHER

With a little bit of planning, going shopping with your young child can turn from an exhausting undertaking into a fun experience that's also rich in opportunities for language learning. One thing to remember is that your child has a limited attention span, and so shopping expeditions need to be relatively short.

Part of the experience is the planning you do together before going to the store. Make a shopping list together, for example. Your child can dictate some of the items you need to buy, while you write them down. This activity helps children associate the spoken word with the written word, and they may begin to notice that certain letters represent certain sounds. For this to happen, you will need to use clear printing and complete words, not the shorthand sort of list most of us routinely prepare. During the actual shopping expedition, your child can then locate items by comparing the words on packages with the words on your list.

When you are writing your grocery list you might group items that go together — fruits and vegetables, dairy items, and so on. Making a simple map together of how the store is laid out can encourage your child to help you put the items in categories by using his knowledge of the store. You can even use the map to organize your shopping list in the order of the aisles where the items are found. (Don't throw the map away with the shopping list when you come home! You can use it each time you go to the same store.) During your shopping expedition ask your child questions, such as "I'm buying apples. Is there another fruit you would like me to buy?" "We're having vegetables for dinner. Shall I buy green peas or green beans?" Putting groceries away when you come home is another opportunity for categorizing. Think aloud, or have a conversation with your child, as you put things away. "First, let's put away all the things that go in the freezer. Now give me all the cold things that go in the refrigerator. I'll put the canned juice and soda in the cabinet. The cookies fit on this shelf."

For many of us, opening the mail is done quickly each day. If you are willing to spend a few extra minutes, however, this task can be turned into a learning activity. Sorting the mail into categories (perhaps magazines, catalogs, bills, junk mail, personal letters, and so on) with your child is one simple possibility. Ask her how she might decide where to put a piece of mail. When the sorting is done, ask which pile she would open first, and show her which pile you would pick. Discuss your choices and why you made them. Let your child pick a piece of mail that looks interesting to her and ask why she chose that piece. What made it look interesting? What does she think might be inside? If she chooses a piece of mail that requires a response, you could work on the response together (this might be the time to introduce that unfortunate fact of life — paying the bills!). Thinking aloud about what mail you will keep and what you will throw away helps your child see how you make judgments about importance or lack of importance.

While this is a fairly simple activity, it promotes a number of language skills: understanding that written language is a way to communicate with others, associating print (specific words and letters) with spoken language, classification, following directions, establishing priorities, and, most important, having a two-way conversation.

PLANNING A PARTY

Is a three-year-old too young to be involved in planning his birthday party? Definitely not. He will probably have lots of good ideas (though some of them may not be very practical!) and those can be the source of opportunities to expand your child's language skills. Just think of all the possibilities for language learning that party planning involves. First, you'll need to make a list of friends and family to invite. As your child thinks of the names of the people he wants to come, he will see you write down each one. He can then help you write out the actual invitations, perhaps adding a drawing or (for the older child) printing some of the letters, or maybe just sticking the stamps on the envelopes. Depending on the age of the child, this is another opportunity for him to associate the spoken word with the appropriate written symbols. Some children of this age already know some of the letters of the alphabet. So, when you write Jane and then later on write John, your child may say that both names begin with the same letter or with J.

Next comes a list of party food and supplies. This, of course, becomes an opportunity to shop together for food, games to play, and party favors to give the guests. Then, on the day of the party, you might write out the guests' names on tags that your child can give to his friends as they come in. Finally, reading birthday cards together and writing thank you notes provide additional chances for expanding language. Your child may contribute only a scribble or a letter to stand for a guest's name, but that is a critical part of the activity. You may also consider having your child make thank you cards rather than using store-bought ones, by taking some of his drawings and cutting them into card-size pieces.

COOKING TOGETHER

It's often difficult to find time to cook together as a family, but an occasional cooking session can be fun and is worth planning for. Select something simple to make that involves only a few ingredients and can be completed in less than half an hour. Baking cookies and making puddings lend themselves to this. Using a packaged mix is probably the easiest, but here is a recipe that is simple and appealing to children.

Coconut Macaroons

Preheat oven to 325° F.
Cover cookie sheets with well-greased parchment paper.
Stir together until well blended $^2/_3$ cup sweetened condensed
    milk, 1 large egg white, 1 ½ teaspoon vanilla, and $^1/_8$ tea-
    spoon salt.
Stir in 3½ cups flaked or shredded coconut.
Drop dough, about a tablespoonful at a time, onto cookie
    sheets.
Bake until brown (about 20–25 minutes).
Let stand until cool, and then peel the cookies from the
    parchment by hand or with a spatula or lifter.

71

Package directions or recipes can be read aloud in their entirety to begin with, and then read step by step as you follow each item. The conversation that you have with your child about the ingredients and the steps for making cookies or pudding is an integral part of this activity. Not only does the conversation support your child's growing understanding of communication, but she will become aware of the importance of following directions and of the fact that directions have to be followed in sequence.

Here are some additional concepts that can be expanded when you and your child cook together:

— First — "What shall we do first?"
— Next — "I'll put butter on the cookie sheets next."
— After — "What do we do after the cookies are brown?"
— Before — "We need to stir everything together before we put in the coconut."
— Last — "What is the last thing we need to do?"

Going to the Library

For some people, the library means dusty books, librarians telling them to be quiet, and people trying to study. While libraries may have been like that at one time, they aren't anymore! Today's libraries have computers, videos, games, and puzzles to borrow, in addition to the usual books, newspapers, and magazines. They are lively, active places, often designed to be interesting to children. Librarians also frequently arrange events such as read-alouds, movies, and storytellings.

Many libraries will let you get a library card in your child's name, even when she's an infant. When she's old enough, she might like to get a new one, and print her name on it herself. Having a library card makes your child a member of the library and connects her to the reading community. In addition to going to the library for special activities, your child can explore books in the children's section. Just looking through books independently is a great activity. If one or two books seem to have special appeal, you can borrow them to read aloud to your child. (And don't forget to visit the adult section to borrow one or two books for yourself.) Showing your child some favorite books from your own childhood is another way to interest her in books and reading. But remember to follow her lead: just because you liked the book, doesn't mean she will.

Using the Media

Television and computers are part of everyday life, even for young children. Despite this widespread availability, however, adults need to take an active role in guiding their young children's media use. Suggestions for viewing specific television programs and using computers are given in the final chapter.

TELEVISION

Most preschool children watch television, but what they watch and how often they watch needs to be up to you. Although many parents are rightfully wary of television programming, in the last several years government intervention has made some improvement in issues of quality and appropriateness. Television stations in the United States, for example, are now required to broadcast a minimum of three hours of educational programming weekly, programs are rated by age appropriateness, and many new TV sets include "V chip" technology that allows blocking of particular programs. Cable channels have added many new programs to compete with those on the large networks. As a result, children's television is much more diverse than it once was and, although cartoons and other animation still dominates, game shows, sports shows, animal shows, how-to shows, and news shows are also widely available. Many of these new shows also make an effort to depict boys and girls equally, and to show a broad representation of cultures and communities.

Television programs for young children appeal to the senses. Bright colors, fast action, fantasy, age-appropriate language, and engaging music all add to the attractiveness of the medium. But this means that television is sometimes mesmerizing. How often have you seen a young child sitting in front of the television set with a glassy-eyed look? Clearly, television is a passive activity. Even though television for children has improved, it remains one-sided communication that provides no opportunity for children to ask questions or make responses. There are things you can you do to make watching television less passive and more of a language-learning experience, however. To begin with, you should try to watch some programs with your child, so that television is not strictly used as a babysitting device. This turns watching television into an activity in which there can be communication. Just as you have a conversation about a story that you have read aloud, so too can you have conversations about television programs. Ask questions like these:

— What did you like about that show?
— Which character did you like the best? The least?
— If you could be a character, which one would you pick? Why?
— Did you like the way the program ended? Why?
— Can you think of a different ending?

Even when your child watches alone, he needs to know that some adult will want to talk about the program — either immediately after it is over or, if that is not possible, at a special time set aside for talking about things done during the day. If you did not see the program, you can ask your child to describe it and tell what he did or did not like about it. Your child might even sketch a picture of something from a television program, and that can be the start of a conversation. The most important thing is to be sensitive to what your child is watching and to try to integrate television watching with other things that are happening in your child's life.

THE COMPUTER

Yes, the computer can be a learning tool, but for young children it may be too much like television to make the investment in hardware and software worthwhile. But if you already have a computer or are considering buying one for the whole family's use, it is certainly true that there is a wealth of software and other computer-based material available for the preschool age group. Many CD-ROMs for children are based either on books or on familiar television programs. Websites appealing to children are also proliferating (but parents should note that many of these sites contain a great deal of advertising that generates the same kind of commercial pressure seen with network television). Clearly, computer-based activities that encourage preschoolers to sit on an adult's lap and to do something together are preferable to those that resemble TV.

Although using the computer can be more active than watching television, many of the same cautions that were noted about television still apply. Again, conversation about what is happening on the computer is a critical part of the experience. Although young children, particularly those who have older siblings, may want to experiment with the computer, parental involvement is essential.

Going on Trips or Outings

Almost all families plan times to do special things together. Visiting family and friends, going on vacation, going to the park for a play date, and taking a trip to the local zoo or children's museum are all opportunities for language learning. Conversations before the special event, lots of talk during the activity, and talking, drawing, or writing afterward will make the experience more fun for everyone, and provide opportunities for language to come alive for your child.

As an example, vacations, even very short ones, involve planning, packing, looking at maps, and figuring out places to stay and things to eat. Young children can be a part of all these activities.

PLANNING

Decide on the dates for the vacation and mark them off on a wall calendar. Your child is likely to ask questions such as "How many days before we leave?" or "How many days will we be away?" These can lead to counting and reading the names of the days of the week. If you have a pet, will that pet be going along or do you have to find someone to take care of it? This is the sort of topic that will start a thoughtful discussion about plans that must be made.

PACKING

Your child can be involved in choosing clothes, toys, and games to pack. Questions such as "Do you want to take your blue or yellow sweater?" can help in learning colors. Talking about the type of clothes that would be best to take (bathing suits and

shorts as opposed to heavy jackets) can help children understand the relationship between the weather and clothing.

LOOKING AT MAPS

Even young children can be told about routes and places they
will pass on the way to a final destination. Getting ready for a
car or airplane trip can involve looking at maps. Show him on
the map the place where you live and how far away you are going. Trace out the route with your finger. Keep in mind that the
scale of the map may be different from others you have used
and the travel distance may seem shorter or longer. What is important is that your child sees you using a variety of print as a
part of your life.

PLACES TO STAY

You can describe the place where you will be staying. Is it the
home of a family member or friend? A one- or two-story motel,
or a high-rise hotel with an elevator? Does it have a pool? Is
there a playground or swings? Will there be many other children there? If you have a brochure or can access pictures from a
website, share them with the child. And, of course, encourage
your child to ask questions about the place. In this way he will
know what to expect and be more comfortable when you arrive.

PLACES TO EAT

Your child can talk to everyone in the family about favorite
foods. While he dictates what he's found out to you, you can
make a list of everybody's favorites, with the name of the person who particularly likes that food next to each item. After the
list is finished, talk about the kinds of places that offer these
foods and whether you will find them on your vacation. For example, will you be eating home-cooked food while staying
with family or friends? Will you be shopping for your own food
and cooking it in a rented apartment or cottage? Or will you be
eating mostly at fast-food places or sit-down restaurants?

Making the Right Choice for You and Your Child

In this chapter we have described a number of activities that adults and three- to five-year-old children can participate in together. All of them encourage the sharing and closeness that are so necessary in the lives of young children, and so enjoyable for parents and caregivers. All of them also provide opportunities for language development. These activities range from everyday experiences such as talking together and watching television, to more planned activities including storytelling, reading aloud, playing games, and traveling. In each of these activities the focus is on providing some learning experiences that will enhance your child's listening, speaking, reading, and writing development.

But not all activities are right for all children. It is crucial to remember that while there are many possibilities, it is up to you to select those activities that are most appropriate for you and your child. Follow her lead and recognize the reality of your own busy life in figuring out the best way to enjoy these activities together.

CARING FOR YOUR CHILD:

A TIME FOR DECISIONS

Ellen, aged 18 months, and Jason, 9 months, are sleeping in their strollers while their mothers chat.

LOUANNE: You know, I've been thinking of going back to work in a couple of months. But I just don't know what we want to do about having someone take care of Ellen.

JOANNA: We're having the same problem. My boss called the other day and wanted a definite commitment about when I would be returning to the office. I'm starting to feel pressured.

LOUANNE: Well, my mother offered to come in every day, but I don't think it's such a good idea. Her thinking about young children is so different from ours, and she's pretty hard to talk to sometimes. I think we need to hire someone who we can talk to about what we think is important for Ellen. But it's so expensive!

JOANNA: I'm leaning more in the direction of a daycare center, where I know there will be professionals taking care of Jason. I've started to look around a bit, and have found a few nearby, right in the neighborhood. I'm planning to visit a couple of them. Do you want to come along?

LOUANNE: No, I don't think so. I worry about Ellen being around a lot of other children — it just seems too chaotic for such a little girl.

All families have to make decisions about the appropriate type of care for their child. These decisions are very personal and vary from family to family. In this conversation, it is clear that both mothers are concerned about the best environment for their children, but they are looking at different solutions that will suit their family circumstances and views of child rearing. As Louanne and Joanna explore the various options that are available to them, it will be important for them to have some general criteria for decision making in mind. What is most important is that the arrangement for childcare be carefully thought out and appropriate to the family situation.

In this chapter we focus on something that is a critical part of many young children's early years — care by individuals other than parents. There are several choices: your child can stay at your home with a caregiver such as a relative, friend, babysitter, or nanny; she can go to a home daycare or an institutional daycare facility; or, at about age three, she can attend a nursery or preschool. Remember, though, that when another person cares for your child, regardless of the arrangement, it is important that he or she understands and shares your philosophy of child rearing, and is dedicated to helping your child learn and grow. Make sure to discuss these issues with the caregiver, whether it is a relative, friend, babysitter, nanny, or daycare provider in a home or institutional setting.

Here are some questions to think about as you read this chapter:

— How do I find and choose an adult to care for my child in my home?
— Is my child ready to be in a group setting?
— Is a home daycare a good option for us, or would an institutional daycare center be better?
— What sort of structure would best suit my child?
— Do I want my child to be in a setting where academics are emphasized?

Choosing a Caregiver

If you have a wonderful, reliable person who has cared for your child in your home since he was born, then just skip this section. If, on the other hand, you are looking for such a person, there are some things to keep in mind. Of course, you will want to find someone who is gentle, kind, reliable, and so on. But, during these early years when children are listening to language, learning to use language, and beginning to expand their vocabulary, it is also important for them to interact with an adult who is verbal — that is, someone who is interested in what your child has to say and can respond appropriately.

One way to find out how a potential caregiver will interact with your child is to schedule some playtime after the more formal interview that you hold. Depending on the age of the child, this playtime can be anywhere from ten minutes to half an hour. The caregiver can play a game with your child, read to her, or interact with her in some other way. Your role in this activity is to observe the communication between your child and the caregiver. Are your child's questions answered? Does the caregiver initiate some of the conversation? Does your child seem to understand the caregiver? Is there give and take in the conversation?

Choosing a caregiver for a young child is a difficult, time-consuming task, and you'll need to rely on your impressions, a check of the caregiver's references, and recommendations from trusted friends and family members. Remember that it's not just your decision, however. If your child is old enough, why not ask him how he felt during the play period? Even a three-year-old can have very astute reactions to a new person.

Selecting a Daycare Facility

If you decide to look for care for your child outside your home, one of the options available to you is a daycare facility that caters to infants and young children. In many communities, there are dozens of such facilities to choose from, some part of corporate chains, others independent, and some connected to religious institutions. Seek out recommendations from friends and family, and look for centers convenient to your home or workplace. When you've identified a few possibilities, make arrangements to visit.

It is almost always required that daycare facilities be licensed by a government body. This means that the facility has been inspected for such things as the ratio of staff to children (this varies depending on the children's age), staff qualifications, and sanitation and safety issues. When you visit a daycare facility, ask to see the license. Also, ask the director whether the facility carries liability insurance.

When you visit the facilities you've identified as possibilities for your child, you need both to ask questions about the program and to spend time observing the activities. Among the questions to ask are the following:

— How many children are enrolled?
— How many children would be in your child's group, and how many staff supervise the group?
— What is the schedule of activities for children your child's age?
— How many staff members are available for different activities?
— May you speak to a parent who has a child of a similar age enrolled?
— If you enroll your child, will you be welcome to drop in for a visit at any time?
— How will the staff communicate with you?

When you spend time in a daycare room, you will want to note things such as these:

— Is the facility clean and attractive?
— Are the children involved with activities that seem right for their age?
— Is there a variety of toys, books, etc., that are appropriate for the children and that your child would enjoy?
— Do the children get individual attention?
— How do the children seem to feel? Are they relaxed? Happy? Bored? Frustrated?
— Is the staff alert and involved with the children?
— Does the staff seem warm and interested in each individual child?
— Does the staff distract those children who seem to be unruly occasionally, interesting them in appropriate activities rather than using punitive measures?
— Is there a sufficient number of staff for the number of children?
— Is there any formal instruction? What is the facility's philosophy on this topic?
— Does the daycare offer before- or after-school care for school-aged children?

Increasingly, questions arise about whether these facilities should be teaching reading and writing. There are many formalized reading programs for very young children. Many of these contain activities of the drill-and-practice type. These programs claim to increase children's reading ability, and research on these types of programs indicates slight short-term reading gains. A problem, though, is that the research also indicates that such programs hamper children socially or emotionally and, furthermore, may hinder the innate desire to learn. Social and emotional development and a desire to learn have been shown to have a long-term effect on children's progress — not only in reading, but in all areas of learning. For this reason, we do not advocate formal reading instruction for children of this age. It is far more important for your child to engage in appropriate activities and experiences based on her interests.Your child will thrive and learn better when she is fully engaged and involved in social interactions than in formal educational activities. As a matter of fact, it is those activities initiated by your child rather than formal direct instruction that promote learning that lasts.

Once you have selected a daycare facility, you need to keep an ongoing relationship with the staff. Drop in occasionally to see how your child interacts with the personnel and the other children. Be sure to read and respond to all notices, letters, or special requests that are sent home. And, most important, observe your child at home to determine the impact of daycare. Children need time to get used to a new environment. If you observe any negative behaviors, such as excessive clinging or aggressiveness, let the daycare center director know about your concerns and work together to solve the problem.

Choosing a Home Daycare

Home daycare facilities — private settings where an adult takes several children into his or her own home to provide care — have proliferated in recent years, and many parents include them in the possible choices for providing care for their children. These facilities vary greatly in terms of training and abilities of personnel, physical settings, and safety. As a result, we advise great caution if you are seeking home daycare for your child. The recommendations of family and friends are of critical importance as you make a decision about a specific homecare facility.

Although some of the same considerations apply to choosing a home daycare or an institutional daycare facility, there are some differences. Home daycare tends to be the responsibility of one individual, rather than a staff. As a result it is very important that you become familiar with the individual who will provide the primary care for your child. In the same way that you would visit an institutional daycare facility, it is essential that you talk with the home daycare provider and see the house. Among the questions to ask are the following:

— Are you licensed? By whom? When does your license expire?
— What is your formal education ? What is your background in early childhood education?
— Are you trained and certified appropriately in first aid and other safety measures?
— Will anyone else be involved in caring for my child on a regular basis? If so, what are his or her qualifications?
— What plans do you have in case of an emergency in which you and the children need to leave the house?
— How many years have you been in operation?
— How many children do you care for?
— What is the age range of the children?
— Are all the children with you all day, or do some arrive before or after school?
— What are the provisions for breakfast, snacks, and lunch? What about naptime?
— Is there an outside play area that is safely fenced and gated?
— Does the ouside play area have safety equipment and turf?
— How frequently do the children use the outdoor facility?
— How will you communicate with me?
— Do you have a set of policies that I can read?

In general, it is more difficult to evaluate a home daycare center than an institutional facility. In many communities, however, a government agency can provide a list of licensed home daycares in your neighborhood, and this can be a good way to start setting up your interviews and visits. We cannot emphasize enough the importance that you consider only regulated, licensed facilities.

Choosing a Preschool

Preschools generally offer programs to children in the last year or two before kindergarten or first grade. Many of the things noted for choosing a daycare facility hold true for choosing a preschool. This is a very personal decision, with a number of aspects. Questions such as the following need to be answered:

— Would you prefer a preschool that is in your neighborhood and caters primarily to neighborhood children?
— Would you prefer a preschool that continues through kindergarten? Through the early grades?
— Would you prefer a preschool that is completely independent, or do you want one that is affiliated with an organization, religious or otherwise?
— Would you prefer a preschool that is organized as a cooperative, in which you will need to be involved and provide services in specific ways?
— Would you prefer a preschool with a diverse enrollment of children from a variety of backgrounds, or one that is more homogeneous?
— Would you prefer a girls- or boys-only preschool, or one that is coeducational?
— Is the school accredited by a professional organization (such as, in the United States, the National Association for the Education of Young Children)?
— What are the backgrounds and experience of the teachers?
— What is the instructional philosophy of the school?
— What are the entrance requirements, if any?
— How does the school communicate with parents?
— Are parents actively involved in developing school policies?
— Are the fees within your budget?

All of these questions are important, and the answers will lead you to investigate different types of facilities. From our perspective, though, one of the most critical factors in selecting a preschool is its openness in allowing you to observe classes

85

over time. Only by being in a classroom can you fully understand the school's instructional philosophy and the program. Observing teachers and children as they interact is the best way to see if a particular preschool is the right one for your child. You know your child better than anyone else, and only you know if your child will do well in a particular environment. For example, if you consider your child to be quiet and shy, you might not want a very hectic environment that may be overwhelming for her. On the other hand, you need to observe how the teacher interacts with a shy child in that environment. Perhaps some additional activity is exactly what your child needs.

As you begin to understand the philosophy of the school and observe the overall program, your focus should include the language and literacy experiences that are provided. The checklist below may be helpful as you observe in the preschool classroom.

THE PHYSICAL ENVIRONMENT

— Is there sufficient space for a variety of activities? Are there separate activity areas?
— Does the room reflect a focus on developing language? Are there large areas for writing, drawing, and painting? Comfortable spaces for looking through books and magazines? Is children's work posted around the room? Are there special interest corners to stimulate conversation (for example, a classroom pet such as a fish or turtle, or a plant corner near a window)?
— Does each child have a special place to store his or her things?

CLASSROOM INTERACTION

— Are there ongoing conversations between teacher and child?
— Are there ongoing conversations among the children?
— Are all the children involved in some activity?
— Does the teacher seem to be attentive to all the children?
— Is there time for children to choose independent activities?

— How does the staff handle probem children who may be aggressive or disruptive? Do they encourage the children to find satisfactory outlets for their behavior?

THE PROGRAM

— Is storytelling a regular activity?
— Does the teacher read aloud every day?
— Are children encouraged to scribble write?
— Are drawing and painting a regular part of the school day?
— Is there an emphasis on speaking and listening to others?
— Do all the children have to participate in the same activity at the same time, or is there a variety of ongoing activities?

Some parents feel that if they send their child to a preschool, it will have a lasting effect on achievement in later grades. This is not necessarily accurate. The research regarding preschool attendance and the benefits on later reading achievement shows varied results. Most studies indicate that achievement in school is improved by early learning experiences, particularly those that emphasize the social and emotional development of children rather than formal academic study. Some studies indicate that formal academic programs in preschool do not produce significant differences in later school achievement. Further, preschool seems to be most beneficial for those children who do not have many playmates of their own age.

Numerous studies, and our own work and experiences, lead us to believe that the decision to send your child to preschool should be based on whether the preschool will enhance your child's social and emotional development, rather than on potential academic factors. That is, you should not make a decision about preschool based on prospects or promises about whether it will help your child be a successful student in the future. Ultimately, though, the decision to send your child to a preschool should be determined by your childcare needs, the level of interaction your child has with adults and other children, and your financial situation.

Choosing What's Right for Your Family

In this chapter we have noted a number of criteria to help you select the best care environment for your young child. The decision to take care of your child yourself, hire a caregiver, ask a member of the family or a friend to take care of your child, or enroll your child in a daycare facility or preschool is a highly personal one. But remember that, with children at this age, you can often make changes and find different arrangements from among the many possibilities available. Watch your child's reactions to the setting you've selected, and keep in mind your own changing circumstances as you make the best choices for you and your family.

FINDING THE RIGHT RESOURCES

FOR YOUR CHILD

Some parents and caregivers are sitting in the library, waiting for a toddler read-aloud program to begin.

PIERRE: There are so many books in the picture book section. I have real trouble trying to figure out which ones are the best.

MARJORIE: I usually just pick out ones that have nice pictures or ones that are in the award-winner section. I see a lot of books that have "Caldecott winner" stickers on them. I guess that's some big prize.

FRAN: That's an award given to books that have great illustrations. I tend to get them, too — but Robbie doesn't seem to be as thrilled with them as I am. I think what I like and what he likes are often different.

PIERRE: Then what do you do? Do you get what he likes, what some award group likes, or what you like?

FATIMA: I usually look on the Web for suggestions, but some of the sites are only advertisements for products. How do we know what's really good?

CAROLINA: It's really overwhelming. I try to pick what's best, but sometimes I need help deciding.

There are no simple solutions to the questions and problems raised in this very common scene. But the single most important factor in deciding what to read with your child or what toys, games, and videos to buy is knowing yourself and your child. As Fran so aptly suggests in her comment, just because something wins an award or is a favorite of yours does not necessarily mean that it is appropriate for your child or that he will enjoy it.

In this chapter we focus on resources that are available for you and your child. As concerned parents bombarded by advertisements for and information about many materials, you may have a number of questions about deciding among them:

— What books should I read to my child?
— What programs should my child be watching on TV?
— How much television is too much?
— Does my child need a computer?
— What toys should I buy to stimulate my child?

The answers to questions like these are important because they will help determine what your young child sees, hears, touches, and plays with during her early years. The remainder of this chapter offers ideas for making decisions, along with specific resource recommendations. These recommendations are not intended to be exhaustive. There are hundreds of fine materials for children available, but only a few can be described here because of space constraints. Our website, www.ladder-to-literacy.com, will be updated frequently to include more suggestions.

Selecting Books

When selecting books for the youngest children, from birth to about age two, look for durability and practicality. Books that are washable — board books with heavy, laminated pages and cloth books — make good choices, since your child may get the book dirty or want to chew on its pages. Books for babies and young toddlers should have simple pictures with not too many things going on. Look for books that activate any of the five senses — materials in different textures, three-dimensional objects, small attached toys such as rattles — can be beneficial in that they enhance the reading experience for these young children.

There are two distinct categories of books for toddlers and preschoolers: simple picture books, and picture storybooks with more fully developed storylines. In the case of picture storybooks, the unity between text and illustration is vital — together they create the experience. (By the way, if you have an older child, remember that picture storybooks are still appropriate; in fact, many are written with the school-aged child in mind.) When selecting books for this age group, you might want to consider these questions:

FOR FICTION...

— Is this book appropriate for my child's age group?
— Is it a good story, one that will interest my child?
— Are the characters well described and developed?
— Is the language engaging, simple, and clear?
— Are stereotypes avoided?
— Do the illustrations help establish the feeling of the story?
— Do the illustrations help to show where the story takes place?
— Are the illustrations appropriate to the level of the book?
— Do the illustrations move the story forward?

FOR NONFICTION...

— Are ideas presented in a logical sequence?
— Is the writing clear?
— Are concepts described using clear illustrations?
— Do the illustrations add to and clarify information?
— Are the illustrations realistic?

As with younger children, choosing books for toddlers and preschoolers should be guided in part by practicality: the book should be well enough made to stand up to repeated readings. Children of this age can also become more actively involved in reading and can begin learning concepts of print and conventions of books. Therefore, you should also consider questions of format when making your decisions:

— Is the size of the book appropriate for a child of this age?
— Can your child hold the book herself?
— Does the cover give some clues to the book's content?

The following section contains some recommendations for you of books that we feel are good choices for particular ages. But remember that these are just suggestions, and are certainly not all inclusive. When selecting from this or any other list, it is most important to keep in mind that you should select books that you and your child will enjoy. Just because a book is recommended by someone or by some source, does not make it a perfect match for you and your child.

Alborough, Jez. *Hug.* Candlewick Press, 2003.
A simple and colorful board book in which all the animals hug each other.

Baby Faces. DK Publishing Inc., 2001.
This adorable board book is filled with photos of babies in action. Some of the words in this book include kissing, laughing, happy, sad and crying.

Cousins, Lucy. *Where is Maisy's Panda?: A Lift-the-Flap Book* Candlewick Press, 2002.
Maisy has lost her favorite toy, Panda, and looks everywhere for him. Flaps lift up as you and your baby look for Panda.

Katz, Karen. *Counting Kisses.* Simon and Shuster Children's Publishing, 2004.
A kiss and read book where babies can count the kisses with you. For example, how many kisses does it take to say goodnight?

Sleepy Bunny. Penk Inc., 2003.
A pat the bunny cloth book. Babies will love to move the Bunny from page to page as Bunny has a snack, puts the toys away, and goes to sleep.

Tong, Willabel. L. *Zoo Faces.* Piggy Toes Press, 1996.
A soft, cuddly cloth book depicting the heads of different animals including an elephant, a giraffe, and a tiger.

BOOKS FOR TODDLERS (ONE TO THREE YEARS)

Base, Graeme. *The Water Hole.* Harry N. Abrams, Inc., 2001.
A delightful book in which wildlife from all parts of the world comes to drink at the water hole until it dries up. As rain replenishes the water hole, all the animals come back.

Berenstain, Stan and Jan Berenstain. *My Potty and I: A Friend in Need.* Random House, 1999.
The Baby Bears show the joys and pitfalls of this toddler-years hurdle by taking a fun-filled lesson in potty training.

Boynton, Sandra. *Dinos To Go.* Simon & Schuster Children's Publishing, 2001.

Seven different dinosaurs dash and play in this lively board book. Toddlers can use colorful picture tabs to choose a dinosaur to read about.

Brown, Margaret Wise. *Goodnight Moon*. Harper Collins Children's Book Group, 2003.
This book has withstood the test of time. It tells a beautiful story of the world going to sleep.

Gikow, Louise. *Bye-Bye, Pacifier*. Random House, 1999.
Baby loves her pacifier, but one day the nanny takes it away. Baby sees the rest of her friends without pacifiers, and realizes that she doesn't need one, either.

Hill, Eric. *Good Night, Spot*. Penguin Putnam Books for Young Readers, 2002.
Spot the dog has a very busy day. Children will enjoy the patterns in Spot's day, and may notice how it mimics their own.

Merritt, Kate. *My Dad*. Sterling Publishing Co., Inc., 2002.
An open-the-flaps book tells the story of a forgetful Dad.

Parr, Todd. *Otto Goes to Bed*. Little Brown Children's Books, 2003.
It is time for bed but Otto, a dog, doesn't want to go. Just like a toddler, he tries all kinds of things before he falls asleep.

My First Body Board Book. DK Publishing, Inc., 2004.
A board book that pictures and labels all the body parts. A fun way for toddlers to find and name the parts of their bodies.

Van Fleet, Matthew. *Tails*. Harcourt Children's Books, 2003.
A delightful animal book in which the animals have tails made of different fabrics. All the tails wag and swish, and can be touched.

Weiss, Ellen. *Bye-Bye, Diapers*. Golden Books, 1999.
Baby Piggy explains how she used to wear diapers, would have to be changed and sometimes got rashes. She decides that she wants to be like the big kids and use the potty.

BOOKS FOR PRESCHOOLERS (THREE TO FIVE YEARS)

Berenstain, Stan and Jan Berenstain. *My Trusty Car Seat: Buckling Up for Safety*. Random House, 1999.

Children can hop aboard for a lesson on safety while they share a baby bears' eye view of a car ride through Bear Country.

Bunting, Eve. *My Big Boy Bed*. Houghton Mifflin Co., 2003.

A three year old with a new bed celebrates all the new things he can do.

Carroll, Lewis. *Alice's Adventures in Wonderland*. Simon & Shuster Children's Publishing, 2003.

A faithful adaptation of the original story, in which flaps and pop-up structures hold a surprise on every page.

Cronin, Doreen. *Diary of a Worm*. Harper Collins Children's Book Group, 2003.

An amusing book about the life of an earthworm family. The Worm whose diary this is wears a red baseball cap, and goes to school and to the dentist, among other places.

Crozon, Alain, and Aurelie Lanchais, *Who Am I?: Wild Animals* Chronicle Books, 2002.

Children can lift colorful flaps in this book to solve riddles and reveal the identity of favorite animals.

Curtis, Jamie Lee. *I'm Gonna Like Me: Letting Off a Little Self Esteem*. Harper Collins Children's Book Group, 2002.

Through the point of view of a boy and a girl, this book shows children that the key to feeling good is liking yourself.

dePaola, Tomie. *Trouble in the Barkers' Class*. Penguin Putnam Books for Young Readers, 2003.

Problems arise when a new student arrives in class. This is the third book of a series featuring Welsh terriers, and looking at the ears of these canine creatures is irresistible.

Fox, Mem. *Koala Lou*. Voyager Books, 1994.

A koala feels very special because of her close relationship with her mother. A great story to read to children who are about to become older siblings to a new baby.

Glaser, Shirley. *The Alphazeds*. Disney Press, 2003.

This visually striking book is done as a one-act play, in which one letter after another enters the stage. Each letter has a distinctive personality.

Henkes, Kevin, *Chrysanthemum*. Harper Collins Children's Book Group, 1996.

Chrysanthemum loved her name — until she went to school, where the other children made fun of her. She learns to be proud of her name and of herself.

Hess, Paul, *Farmyard Animals*. Zero to Ten, Ltd., 2003.

Simple words and exquisite pictures of animals make this book a treasure.

Lewis, J. Patrick, *Doodle Dandies: Poems That Take Shape*. Simon & Schuster Children's Publishing, 1998.

A collection of poems that literally take the shape of the subject at hand.

Lionni, Leo, *The Alphabet Tree*. Alfred A. Knopf Inc., 2004.

This special tree houses the letters of the alphabet. After a storm, a bug and a caterpillar teach the letters how to become words, and eventually a sentence!

London, Sara, *The Good Luck Glasses*. Scholastic, 2001.

Nomi decides she is lucky when her new glasses help her to see more clearly.

Martin, Jr. Bill. *Brown Bear, Brown Bear, What Do You See?* Henry Holt & Company, 1996.

A classic picture book with a rhyming structure that allows children to predict easily the next lines and to join in the reading.

Mayer, Mercer. *I Am Sharing*. Random House, 1995.

A cooperative little critter shows how he shares everything — except for the television, when his favorite show is on.

McGuire, Leslie. *Brush Your Teeth, Please*. Reader's Digest Association, 2003.

This pop-up book shows children how animals brush their teeth and how they should, too.

Provensen, Alice. *A Day In the Life of Murphy*. Simon and Shuster Children's Publishing, 2003.

Murphy, a terrier, goes through a complete day from early morning to bedtime with his family.

Ray, Mary Lyn. *All Aboard!* Little, Brown Children's Books, 2002.

The book tells the story of a little girl's first trip away from home. She is off to see her grandparents and takes her toy rabbit, Mr. Barnes, as a companion.

Steptoe, John, *Baby Says*. Harper Collins Children's Book Group, 1988.

A baby charms his big brother as they spend time together.

Taback, Simms, *There Was an Old Lady Who Swallowed a Fly*. Penguin Books Canada, Ltd., 1997.

This classic story has a very sing-song style. Many would think of it as a basic nursery rhyme.

Turner, Sandy. *Otto's Trunk*. Harper Collins Children's Book Group, 2003.

Otto, the elephant, is tired of being teased about his tiny trunk, and tries without luck to make it bigger. Children who feel shortcomings of their own will relate to Otto.

Uegaki, Chieri. *Suki's Kimono*. Kids Can Press, 2003.

Suki's grandmother comes to visit from Japan and brings her a kimono. Suki wears her new kimono to the first day of school with unhappy results at first.

Viorst, Judith. *Alexander and the Terrible, Horrible, No Good, Very Bad Day*. Simon & Shuster Children's Publishing, 2002.

Alexander has a terrible day when one thing after another goes wrong for him.

For additional recommended titles, visit our website at www.ladder-to-literacy.com. We also suggest that you consult other sources for recommendations, including preschool teachers, children's librarians, and neighbors, friends, and relatives with children similar in age to your own. There are also many organizations that produce useful booklists: for example, the American Library Association lists the winners and runners-up for the Caldecott Medal for outstanding illustration at its website (www.ala.org); the International Reading Association makes its annual Children's Choices and Teachers' Choices booklists available at its website (www.reading.org/choices/).

Using Television and Video

Children of all ages need to be active participants in varied experiences. Too often, children are engaged in passive activities such as watching a video, DVD, or television program. A young child's daily life should involve time for outdoor and indoor play, rest, and activities with others, and there should not be long unfilled periods when the child gravitates towards the TV set. That is not to say that watching television or videos is inherently bad, but it should not be used as a babysitter. Parents and other caregivers should also find ways to use television appropriately. Parents need to take control of the television and videos that their children view. You can screen what you allow your child to watch and guide her toward selections that are age and content appropriate. And consider limiting the time you allow your young child to watch, since excessive viewing has been shown to have detrimental effects on health and development.

Parents and caregivers should watch programs with their children. Young children enjoy having adults laugh with them and explain what is going on when explanations are needed. Talking with your child while viewing can help build critical thinking and problem-solving skills, while encouraging creativity. You can discuss the good choices and bad choices that television characters make. You can heighten your child's observational skills by asking questions about the characters and the story: Why did you think that was funny? Did you like the music that they played? Why is this your favorite show? Why were they having a party? What happened when Bert didn't share? What do you think would have happened if he did share? Discuss what's real and what's not with your child.

Television and videos can spark interest in reading books about things seen on television. There are many books tied to TV shows; The Magic School Bus, Arthur, and Barney series are just a few. After you've watched an interesting show, you can follow up by visiting the library to find books from which the program was adapted, additional stories by the authors of those specific books, or books on the show's topic. Although there are an increasing number of quality television programs for children of all ages, you have more control if you explore some of the many excellent videos and DVDs designed to entertain and to educate young children. You can often find good choices to borrow or rent from local libraries or video stores, or you can build a library of videos of your own for repeated viewing. Yard sales are often a good source for slightly used tapes.

Computers and the Internet

Many parents feel that it is necessary to purchase a computer for their young children, but we believe that the expense outweighs the benefits. There are simply not very many software programs that actively engage very young children, and by the time your child is really ready for a computer, the computer that you purchased when your child was very young will be obsolete.

Although we do not advocate the use of computers with children of this age, we do recognize that parents often want to expose their children to technology early on. If you already have a computer, you might want to introduce it to your child when he is three or four. You may want to purchase software aimed at this age group. As with other media discussed in this chapter, finding software for your child involves knowing the media and knowing your child. The following list contains some criteria to consider when purchasing software for young children:

— The software should be developmentally appropriate for the age of the child.
— The software should require active participation, conversation, and creative play.
— The software should have excellent visuals and sound.
— Instructions should be spoken rather than written.
— Where appropriate, instant feedback should be provided to the child. If a child is supposed to "answer" something in the program, the software should be designed so that your child gets an immediate response.
— The child should be able to control the difficulty and the pace.

If you do use a computer and are connected to the Internet, there are thousands of websites intended for parents and caregivers, as well as children. As previously noted, some of these are commercial sites which tend not to be objective. There are some general guidelines to use in searching out information from the Web, whether at parenting, educational, or other sites. When considering advice, recommendations, suggestions, or resources from the Web, always look at the credibility, objectivity, and accuracy of the site. Set aside ample time to visit multiple sites, since no single site will provide you with comprehensive information. We suggest that for educational or parenting tips, you visit at least four reputable sites. Be sure to find out who runs the site. What are their qualifications, credentials, affiliations, and professional experience? Consider the source of the information: it is vitally important to be aware of the sponsor of the site. If it is a commercial site, you need to screen the information carefully in order to ensure that it is objective and not just geared to selling a product.

The following are some basic questions to consider:
— Who is the producer or author of the webpage?
— Is the author easy to identify?
— Is the page sponsored by a reputable organization?
— Is there an address and phone number on the page, in addition to an e-mail address?
— Is the site free of any biases?
— Are all sides of a problem presented?
— Is the site free of distortions or outrageous claims?
— Is this a commercial site that is trying to sell you something?
— Are sources listed for any data presented?
— How does information from the site compare to other sources?
— Is the page updated regularly?

Games and Toys

When deciding on games and toys for children of any age, it is important to keep in mind the developmental age and individual interests of the child. Good toys are appealing to the child and appropriate for her stage of intellectual, physical, and social development. It is also vital to ensure that the toys and games are safe and durable: you don't want to buy something that a child can easily break or something that will quickly fall apart.

Toys for very young children (birth to nine months) should promote their interest in looking, listening, touching, grasping, and tasting. Crib mirrors, rag dolls, stuffed toys, and simple hand puppets you can move are all age appropriate. Be especially sure that they meet all safety regulations for infants and toddlers, and that there have no small pieces that could go into your child's mouth. Infants from nine months to one year of age enjoy bath toys, construction materials, simple puzzles, cloth and board books, and balls.

The new mobility and increased independence of the young toddler make him interested in different toys and games. Toys that engage him in dressing and lacing are particularly enjoyable. In addition, toys and games that involve stringing things and stacking materials are often favored. At this age, children love to draw and scribble, so nontoxic crayons or markers and lots of paper should be made available.

Three- to five-year-olds love to pretend, and they delight in dress-up clothes. You don't have to purchase anything special — any of your old clothes or accessories will suffice. Be sure, though, that they are safe. Be careful about long beaded necklaces or anything else which might prove a danger to your child. Blocks and simple card or board games are also enjoyed by three- to five-year-olds.

Young children naturally respond to rhythm, and exposing them to music and song during these early years can promote language development, creativity, and social interaction. If you don't play a musical instrument or have one in your home, you and your child can sing songs, beat out rhythms, or simply relax and listen to music together. Music can contribute to a soothing environment for infants and toddlers. Rattles, drums, and shakers can be enjoyed — and they help develop motor skills. Instruments can be created by using blocks, spoons, pots and pans, empty plastic containers, and coffee cans.

Children of all ages love blocks and often continue to use them as they grow. Infants and toddlers enjoy touching and gripping large, textured blocks. Toddlers like to stack, combine, or line up blocks. Children who are a bit older begin to recognize designs and patterns and often delight in building different structures.

Jigsaw puzzles provide children with experiences that foster language skills and help them solve problems and coordinate their thoughts and actions. Look for puzzles that are age appropriate and durable: Puzzles that are well made can be used for many years. For the youngest children, look for those with just a few pieces and be sure that the pieces are large enough so that they cannot be swallowed. Two-year-olds may simply enjoy putting pieces in and taking them back out without much thought or care as to whether they are in the right spots.

As your child begins to use scissors and glue, you can create your own puzzles. He can cut pictures from magazines or you can take your child's drawings and mount them on sturdy cardboard. Cover the pictures with clear contact paper to make them more durable. Then, mark and cut out puzzle pieces on the picture, mix the pieces up, and reassemble them.

Children of all ages delight in water play. Puddles, spray bottles, garden sprinklers, water tables, and wading pools fascinate young children and foster many learning experiences. It is important to remember that young children don't mind getting messy or wet; in fact, they often delight in it. Save some old clothes so that they have ample opportunities to be messy and get dirty or wet without fear that they are ruining good clothes. Parents and caregivers must, however, be extremely diligent when supervising children in water, whether a bath or a wading pool. Remember that a young child can drown in water as shallow as one inch.

Above all, it is important to know that good toys are not necessarily expensive, and children do not need very many. Rotate toys and games by putting selected ones away for a while. If a toy is put away for a month or two and then brought out, it will seem new to her, and will provide new opportunities and experiences for your child.

Young children learn by doing things. They should be active participants in a variety of experiences that engage them in exploration and interaction with others. Young children learn best by seeing, hearing, touching, tasting, smelling, and moving their bodies. Acivities that spark their imagination, stimulate talk, and generate opportunities for self-expression are very beneficial. Children should be provided with and use a wide variety of experiences, games, books, videos, toys and other activities that have them doing things. By being active participants in age-appropriate activities, children will begin to embrace learning.

AFTERWORD

Throughout this book, we have tried to provide clear-cut examples of ways to enhance your child's reading and writing. We feel that parents and caregivers can and should be the first link to literacy for young children. We also know that parents today are often busy, overworked, and overloaded. We do not want to add to that stress; rather, we designed this book with the mindset that through simple everyday occurrences, parents and caregivers can greatly facilitate early learning.

Our website, www.ladder-to-literacy.com, will be continually updated with recommendations of new books, games, videos, and resources. It has a discussion board and an area for questions and answers, so we hope it will become a place where readers of this book can communicate with us and with the larger community of people who are interested in young children and the development of literacy.

When we originally designed this book, we envisioned one volume that dealt with children from birth up to early adolescence. Our publisher encouraged us to break it out into two books. The next book, *A Leg Up: Enhancing a Child's Reading and Writing*, follows the school-age child. We hope that you have found this book to be informative, helpful, and readable, and that you will follow us into the next book to continue discussing reading and writing as your child grows up.